Doctor in War and Peace
the Memoir
of
Thomas Henry Wilson Esquire

Spire Publishing -April 2011

First published in Canada and the UK 2011
by Spire Publishing Ltd.

A cataloguing record for this book is available from the
Library and Archives Canada.
Visit www.collectionscanada.ca/amicus/index-e.html

Book, cover and all illustrations designed by Sharon Wilson
swilson@videotron.ca
Montreal, Canada

www.spirepublishing.com
Printed and bound in the USA or the UK
by Lightning Source Ltd.
ISBN: 978-1-926635-47-7

TABLE OF CONTENTS

CONTENTS CONT'D

Acknowledgements

The sound archive department of The Imperial War Museum carried out the interview, and gave permission to make a typescript of the sound interview for use in this book, for which many thanks.

I am profoundly grateful to Dr. John Surtees for his advice on content, and knowledge of the publishing world.

I am grateful too for the advice and help given by Michael Partridge, of the Old Eastbournian Association.

I appreciate input from Geoffery Cooper, who worked closely with my father at the Chasely Home, and became a good friend of him.

I have enjoyed and appreciated the knowledge and advice of Christina Manolescu who first opened my eyes to the world of self-publishing and has since been a consultant.

I am very grateful for the advice and help of Sharon Wilson (no relation) for her work and ideas in putting together graphics and illustrations, having herself also published a book.

Foreword

This book is the publication of the life of Tom Henry Wilson, basically in words he dictated in 1990. It describes his life from his earliest days as the son of a London doctor, through his own medical training towards qualifying and starting practice in Eastbourne.

His career was interrupted by the beginning of the Second World War, at which time he went to France in February 1940 with the Royal Army Medical Corp, and became a prisoner of war when the field hospital where he was operating was overrun by German forces.

He only returned to England in May of 1945 (actually crossing the coast on what became VE Day, May 8)

The story of his 5 years as a POW is depicted in the typescript of an interview with staff of the Imperial War Museum.

The book's editor, Tom's son Crichton, has added a few notes and corrections, and in particular has added some sections on Tom's life as a surgical consultant after the war in Eastbourne, and about some personal aspects of his life, including his love of tennis.

The little girl in the middle on the tricycle is Edith Boxer, later to become Tom's mother. The photo was taken in 1880.

Family Life

I, Thomas Henry Wilson, was born on the 28th November 1904, nearing midnight (so I am told) at Rose Cottage, in the village of Antony, a few miles inland from Torpoint, in the county of Cornwall.

My father was Thomas Wilson and he was posted to the nearby Fort Tregantle at the end of the Boer War, where he had enlisted as a surgeon to the British Army in South Africa. He was brought up in Ballymena, Ulster, in Northern Ireland, and trained as a medical student at Trinity College, Dublin, eventually becoming a Fellow of the Royal College of Surgeons in Ireland. I never knew anything about his family, but I can remember meeting his brother when I was young - a tall six footer. I remember my father returned to Belfast to bury his parents, but we were never taken with him.

My mother, Edith Mary Crichton Wilson (née Boxer) was the first-born and only daughter of Captain James Alfred Boxer, RN, and his wife. There were three sons born later, Arthur, Hubert, and Henry. Hubert entered the Bank of England, but Arthur and Henry entered the Royal Navy to carry on the old tradition. There is a large family tree of the Boxer family, going back centuries.

I believe that my parents met at a Service social function in Plymouth, where there were many of the Boxer family still serving in the Navy. They were married at Christ Church, Folkestone, Kent. Grandpa Boxer had been superintendent of the South Eastern & Chatham Railway Harbour there before he retired. He lived at No 1 Marine Parade, next to the harbour and the Pavilion Hotel. The wedding was on 3 January 1904 and the reception was at the Wampach Hotel, behind the Leas. There are some splendid photographs still of this event.

Rose Cottage was a lovely little one, opposite the village public house, the Ring of Bells. I have a photo of this cottage taken by myself. On this trip I called at the cottage and the lady who answered the door remembered my birth and pointed out the upper right hand window of the room.

I was christened at the Church in Antony on Christmas Day 1904, also shown in the photograph. I am told that we only stayed there for six months. Father 'put up his plate' - Thomas Wilson, Physician and Surgeon - at No 185 Chevening Road, Brondesbury, London, NW6. In those days, this was the usual custom and you stayed at home waiting and hoping that a prospective patient would arrive! This was a cozy semi-detached house of two floors. The front room ground floor was large with a bay window behind a room used as the consulting room, while the kitchen quarters were down a long passage, which also led to the garden. The garden overlooked the North London Railway and was quite exciting for children. A new synagogue was built opposite us.

After a few years we moved over the road to a semi-detached end house, No 108, of a long row of houses. This was a bigger and better house on a corner of the roads and overlooked Queens Park.

As a family we returned to Antony the next year and I believe I can remember wandering off from a picnic party and getting lost by going to sleep in a cornfield, but was eventually found. Whether I really remember this at eighteen months or put a memory picture on being told the story later, I cannot say, but the path and the cornfield are still vivid in my 'memory'. I later had two brothers, William Hubert, born 22 May 1909, and Aubrey Joseph, born 22 September 1913. I don't think we were very close, for four years is quite a gap. We all eventually went to school in Cavendish Road (the other side of the railway and nearer the Kilburn High Road). This was a large house with semi-basement and three floors, with a long garden reaching to the same railway. I refer to this school as a 'Marm's School'. The headmistress, Mrs. Plummer, was tall elegant, well-educated and strict but she did ensure that we were given a good grounding education.

When I was about 10 or 11, I was taken to the City of London, to Merchant Taylors' School, in Charterhouse Square, EC1, to sit the examination for a scholarship, so they must have thought I knew something. This went on for several days, till one day I was presented with a Latin paper. Consternation - because I had never been taught any Latin. The presiding master realized I was not writing and came to talk to me and on hearing the facts he let me go home. I believe that after the first day, I travelled alone on the Bakerloo and Metropolitan lines, from Queens Park, via Baker Street, to Aldersgate Street station (now re-named the Barbican).

Of course, they couldn't give me a scholarship without my knowing any Latin, but they decided I knew enough to let me start the next term in the very bottom form, the Lower First Form, where a Mr. Bathhurst (a cricketer) proceeded to teach me Latin. I think that was October 1915. I gradually crept up the school to the Sixth Form till I left in December 1923, just aged 19.

Merchant Taylors' School is run by the Merchant Taylors' Company, one of the livery companies of the City of London, with its own Hall in Threadneedle Street, which was severely damaged in the bombing of London by the German Luftwaffe in World War II. The original school was next to the Old Bailey in Suffolk Lane, but moved to Charterhouse Square when the original Charterhouse School moved to

Godalming, Surrey.

After I left school, Merchant Taylors' also moved to near Rickmansworth, in Hertfordshire, where it remains. The buildings and land of Charterhouse Square were bought for the Medical School of St. Bartholomew's Hospital.

The buildings were huge - stone steps leading up to a large entrance hall and classrooms radiating everywhere on several floors. There was an enormous Hall, which easily held the pupils and staff (over 450). This beautiful hall was also bombed in World War II and was not rebuilt. I have a splendid etching of this hall and the entrance steps on my wall, which I picked up in an antique shop in Seaford about 20 years ago.

There were also cloisters and a beautiful chapel, which the school used on special days, and attendance was compulsory. The ground was square, with a centre plot of grass, but not big enough to enable rugger to be played - only used for practice and cricket nets. There was also a big gymnasium, controlled by an ex-Army Master-at-Arms, who taught us everything from boxing, fencing and gymnastics. He himself, though no longer a youngster, was superb on the bars and with the sword.

School started daily, including Saturday mornings, at

9 a.m. with everyone, including masters, in the Great Hall, when prayers were said by the headmaster, Dr. Nairm, DD, after which he gave out any special news. At 9.15 we started classes in the various rooms. There was the junior school with Lower and Upper First, and Lower and Upper second forms. After that, the school was divided into Classical and Modern forms and later into special forms for Science. I progressed steadily up the lower school, finding that, apart from starting Latin from scratch, my grounding from my Marm's school was well ahead of other boys.

The masters were reasonable fellows, particularly my first form master in the Lower First. After that, most of the younger masters were away fighting in World War I and the locums were elderly and brought back from retirement. I didn't do very well anywhere. However, there was one master who terrified most boys, named Fryer - a sadist, as I now know, unmarried and probably a homosexual, as I discovered later. He ran a form on the Modern side, so I decided to escape him and went on the Classical side. Whilst I must have learned some classics, so poorly taught that I do not remember any of it now - a pity, because when you travel, especially to Italy or Greece, historic knowledge is so helpful.

When I eventually reached the Fifth form level, I again opted to transfer to the Science side, because by then I had decided to become a medical 'doctor' and these were the subjects necessary to pass exams. I spent several very happy years on the science side, where the subjects interested me greatly and the teachers were far better at teaching and explaining things. The time came when I had to take exams and the particular one was the London Matriculation, which, when passed, gave you an entrée to a University and later a degree.

My chemistry master, a Mr. Simpson, when hearing that I had entered my name for this exam when I was 16, ventured to say in front of the class that I 'would never pass'. How correct he was, because the exam consisted of compulsory subjects, English and mathematics, a language (I took Latin), and two science subjects - physics and zoology. I only passed in mathematics.   Mr. Simpson was nice enough to apologize to me in front of the class for his original remark, and he also said he thought I should have done better.

Nothing daunted, I took the Matriculation exam again - and passed in maths and the two science papers. Limited success.   Thereafter, I re-sat the exam every six months, but by the time I left school in December 1923, I had sat five times and failed each time, the last twice in English.   To complete the sorry story, I had some private English lessons from one of my father's patients - studied at home and sat for the sixth time in January 1924.

As I wanted to get on, as a precaution I took another

exam - The College of Preceptors - taking many more subjects, but the ones which would enable me to start in a medical school. Somehow, I passed.

Early in 1924 my father took me to see the Dean of the Medical School at St. Thomas' Hospital, opposite the Houses of Parliament. I elected to try there because from the Science side at Merchant Taylors' School, there was an annual scholarship to St. Thomas', and so many of my friends had won this and were already there.

Now, the Dean was Sir Cuthbert Wallace, FRCS, and another Irishman, so my father and the Dean had lots to talk about, while I was left looking out of the window. Finally, it was agreed that I could start at the bottom of the Medical School in the March term of 1924, with the exam which I had already passed - but of course this could not lead to a university degree.

Sometime before March, the Matric results came out and as on previous occasions, I took out my bicycle and rode to South Kensington, the London University headquarters, to look at the printed results of the exams. I knew exactly where to look from previous experiences, and again my name was not on the list.

So I pedaled home (mostly uphill) very dejected, and told the family the sad news at lunch time. However, later in the day, I started to receive telegrams of congratulations on at last having passed the

Matriculation. Some were pleasant, others were sarcastic, but all meant the same. So back again I cycled to South Kensington - and still I could not see my name. So I looked at other lists and to my surprise I found my name among those who had passed 'First Class'. Unbelievable! I forget how, or even if, we celebrated, because my father ran a busy practice single handed, and there was no time to go out anywhere

My earliest recollection of the family is that we lived at 185 Chevening Road, Brondesbury, London, NW6. This is a long road running east to west, parallel with the old North London Railway, from Brondesbury Park station to Kensal Rise station. No 185 was on the north side and its garden reached the railway just west of the station platform. The house was semi-detached, with the gate to the back garden on the west side. There was a small front garden with a path to the front door. The back garden was long and narrow, mostly of grass. The house was on two floors, ground and upper. On the ground floor in front was the large lounge (or drawing room) and behind was the dining room, while down the passage led to a kitchen and scullery. The upper floor had a large main bedroom in front, a smaller room over the door area, and several small bedrooms on the side and at the rear, plus toilet and bathroom. No central heating in those days. My father used one room as a consulting room and the lounge as a waiting room; somewhere he had a dispensary for medicines.

I can remember my mother holding 'At Home' days, when friends could call to chat and have tea and cakes. In the summer, the garden was used and croquet played. Opposite the house, it was interesting to watch the building of a new synagogue.

After a few years, the chance came to move to a bigger house on the south side of the road. This was no 108. It was the west end of a short terrace of houses, next to the synagogue, and therefore semi-detached. A road ran south here, separating the house from the public park, called Queens Park. The road was Kingswood Avenue.

No 108 was double-fronted, with a large hall and large rooms in front on either side of the hall and another large room on the west side. The front room was my father's consulting room, the other front room was used as a dining room, and a waiting room for his patients. The rear room was a lovely drawing room. All had open fireplaces. At the rear of the hall, three steps led down to a large kitchen, while a further three steps led to the scullery, toilet and a room used as a dispensary. The stairs were in two phases, with a large half landing, with a toilet and two rooms overlooking the back garden, and used for staff living-in.

The upper floor had two big bedrooms in front, with a dressing room between, while there was another large room on the west, overlooking the garden and

Queens Park. This was used as a nursery. The bathroom was also here. There was also a fourth room at the back used by the two elder of us boys as a bedroom. The front garden had a central path and grass on either side with flower beds to edge the grass. There were some lovely flowering trees, such as laburnum and cherry. A path led by the side of the house to the back garden, again with grass and flowerbeds, with a greenhouse. There was a garden gate into a small road running behind the terrace.

In 1909 my brother William Hubert was born. It was in this house, No 108, that I grew up, first going to a small school and later to Merchant Taylors'. In 1913 my second brother, Aubrey Joseph, was born. We used Queens Park a lot, at first with a nanny, but later on our own. We joined in games with other local lads, cricket in particular.

Mother was a keen and good lawn tennis player. For years, we had to go to Gladstone Park, the other side of Willesden Green, at least a two mile walk each way, to play at her tennis club, of which she was often the ladies champion. Father was not a games player, though he tried occasionally wearing in those days long white trousers, a blazer, a tie, and a straw hat. We boys were left to our own devices as we grew up. There was also a cricket club in the same area and we used to watch the games there.

Mother thought nothing of walking to Whiteleys in

Queens Road, Kensington, with a push chair and one, two or three of us with her - perhaps three miles each way, all this in between looking after father and his patients, and supervising the cooking. I believe in the pre-First War days we had a cook and parlour maid, so there was some spare time. In those days, people walked or bicycled - no cars. There was Uncle AB Boxer, who lived in Acton, a bank manager at the Westminster Bank in Kilburn at one time, who thought nothing of walking to see us and back, though he could have taken the North London railway to Willesden Junction and then a tram.

Tom and Edith (nee Boxer) Wilson with sons
(*l to r*) Tom, Joe, and Bill.

Edith Wilson with (*l to r*) Bill, Joe and Tom
taken approximately 1920

Early Military Career

I suppose I started my service career as a very small boy when my mother always dressed me and my two brothers in sailor suits when we went to any particular function, especially family weddings.

The next stage was when I was a schoolboy at Merchant Taylors' School in the City of London, which one joined when one reached the age of 13+, fitting in with the start of a new year in September. One was more or less forcibly made to join the Officers Training Corps. You were fitted out with a uniform consisting of a tunic, riding breeches, puttees and boots followed by webbing equipment, belt and pack, shoulder straps, haversack, water bottle, and bayonet holder. We were fortunate in that the unit was affiliated to the London Rifle Brigade and therefore we had black buttons, and this made it much easier when you had to clean your equipment, but of course the equipment all had brass edges to the buckles, etc. and they had to be cleaned anyway. I think there is a photograph in the album of me and certainly one brother in this OTC uniform and we must have looked rather puny because the war was still on in '17 or '18 and we had to travel to school certain days of the week in uniform to attend parade at school after school hours.

I must say that when one got used to it, it wasn't all that bad, and each year we had an annual camp and I remember the first one I attended was at Mytchett where there was a lovely lake in which we used to bathe regularly. The RAMC Headquarters are now on the other side of this lake, which is joined up to the Basingstoke canal; it is thoroughly septic and bathing is inadvisable.

As the years went by I was promoted to Corporal in charge of No 16 Section of the 4th Platoon and after that to the Sergeant in charge of the 4th Platoon. I never reached the giddy height of Under Officer as many of my close friends did, because I had a contretemps with a sadist schoolmaster, John Fryer, who, although he was only second in command to a Major Davis, who came back from the war with a MC, really seemed to make the decisions. This all arose because at the end of the summer term it was decided to hold some sort of map reading exam which clashed with the school swimming sports. I pointed it out to the master in charge and imagined he would pass it on to my senior in the OTC.

I attended the swimming sports and enjoyed it as usual, doing quite well as I was a reasonable swimmer and represented the school. When I came back the next term, which was in September for the autumn term, I was promptly sent for to the Orderly Room and demoted from Sergeant in charge of the Platoon to Corporal in charge of No 16 Section. They would not listen to reason and I just had to lump it. In spite of this we won the competition for cups, which we (No. 16 Section) carried off with flying colours. This was judged by a regular army officer.

When I left school I went to St. Thomas' Hospital Medical School in March 1924. I was soon approached by one of the non-commissioned officers in the medical section of the University of London Officers Training Corps, and although at first I jibbed and said I had enough of OTCs, I eventually succumbed and joined it, - that is, the St. Thomas' Hospital Medical School Section, ULOTC. Many of my friends also joined and during the time I was with them we really had many enjoyable field days and camps together. I was eventually promoted and as I became more mature, I finished up as a Staff Sergeant in the St. Thomas' Company of the ULOTC.

I had qualified in 1929 and was advised by my commanding officer, Col Mitchiner, consultant surgeon, to take out a commission and take his place as the commanding officer of the St. Thomas' Hospital Unit. This I did, and I carried on until I had done my turn as Senior Registrar at St. Thomas' Hospital, and decided to move to Eastbourne to become a consultant surgeon there.

One started as a full lieutenant in the RAMC and after a year one automatically became a captain. After this I took the major's exam and passed and was due for my majority when I was in Eastbourne.

When in the Medical Unit, we had some delightful camps, and at these camps all the units from all the teaching hospital medical units joined together to form one big collection to make several companies of the Field Ambulance. In those days it was still horse-drawn and we actually practised stretcher drill on an old horse-drawn field ambulance way back from the First War. I well remember my very first camp because our arrival was delayed for a few days as we were all taking our second MBBS exam. This camp was at Felixstowe on Landguard Common and, if you know this common, it is nothing more than shingle, the same as the Crumbles in Eastbourne. All the friends who had taken the exam arrived together by train at Felixstowe and had to march to the camp with our kitbags, and we were detailed to various tents which had already been up for some time. It so happened that that night a terrible storm blew up with lashing rain and very high winds, and as you can imagine the tent pegs did not hold in shingle under those conditions. Our particular tent with, I think, eight people, spent the night keeping each other as happy as possible telling stories by candlelight, and periodically one of us in rotation would strip completely, dash out of the flap, bang in all the tent pegs and hope they would last for another few minutes. Ours was one of the tents that did not fall down.

Another amusing fact was that at some time about 2am, the commanding officer, this Col Mitchiner, came round to everyone and beat on our particular tent and said 'if you want to, you can go over the road to the Girls' School'. There were loud cheers and everyone started to get ready in a hurry, but he said 'No need to hurry because the girls are all on holiday'. Anyhow we had had enough of this rotten night, so our particular tent made sure our belongings were as watertight as possible, took what was necessary and dashed across the road to the girls' school. I don't remember much about the rest of the night. I don't even remember if we had a bed, but I expect we did. Next morning we were all called out on parade and the storm had passed. We then had about a two mile route march to warm up and dry off, all around close to the RAF station. I think most of this now is a part of the Felixstowe Port.

We had other very good camps. Another I remember well was in the Isle of Wight, because no sooner had we arrived at Sandown on a Saturday night in July 1934 than I got a telegram to say that my wife had gone into labour and could I return as soon as possible. Well, as you can imagine, it was not possible. I reported to the CO who gave me permission to go if and when I could. But of course everything shuts up between the island and the mainland at nightfall. I had to wait until next morning before I could get a boat back from Cowes to the mainland, and then back to London, where I arrived a day late but in time to see mother and daughter flourishing at an address, 6 Reynolds Close, Golders Green, on the edge of Hampstead Heath.

Sport

My mother was a great sportswoman in her day. She was a keen tennis player and a member of a well-known tennis club in the Willesden area and used to come home with a lot of trophies after the tournaments. My father was not a sportsman in the sense of the word although he tried to play tennis, and later golf with a limited amount of success. I suppose any skills I had were partly inherited from my mother.

We had a small garden in our house in Chevening Road and I expect we used to play ball with each other as boys, and the parents when they had time to spare. As we grew up I am sure that some stumps were bought and a cricket bat and we played with a soft ball, although later when we got to school age, we certainly used a hard ball – a proper cricket ball - and the garden suffered badly. It had a wooden fence which was always getting hit from the inside and broken, as well as there being a big greenhouse fairly close to what would be the pitch, and that suffered a lot. As I think I said before, next door to our house was Queens Park and the large playing fields there were used by all kinds of people to play all sorts of games in winter and summer, although the park keepers at that time were pretty strict on what they allowed you to do and how belligerent you could get.

In this park we certainly played cricket. We used the tracks for running events, but there were no public tennis courts.

When I went to my public school at Merchant Taylors' in Charterhouse Square in the City of London at age eleven, I certainly had a smattering of cricket, and there of course it was the game in the summer term. In the winter rugby football was played and at all times hand fives. Also at all times there was a very good gymnasium and this was part of the school curriculum, apart from any volunteer things you did after school hours.

Fives

If we take the simpler things first, hand fives was played on an outdoor court with only a very low back wall and while you could play this with bare hands, it paid off to have a pair of fives gloves, when your hands did not suffer so much, and gave you a better shot. For the bigger boys, they had indoor fives courts and of course the school played matches against other schools. This is a good game. You can play it at all ages and when your hand got hardened, it did not suffer at all, and you could play it at all times of the year. I never reached any team events in that sport.

Gymnastics

The gymnasium was very well stocked with equipment and we had two excellent gym masters, the senior being a certain Captain Palmer, who was obviously army trained, with badges all over his vest, and he was an absolute master with the sword. Being fairly elderly to us, he didn't exert himself a great deal at boxing and the more energetic sports, but was a very good teacher. He was assisted by a younger man, also army trained, and when you saw the younger one on the parallel and the horizontal bars, you name it, he was really quite terrific.

Every class in the school had to attend a compulsory session once a week unless you were medically unfit, and that had to be confirmed by the school doctor, who incidentally was a funny little man with a goatee beard, who had his consulting rooms in Charterhouse Square. Nobody ever took him very seriously, but of course his word was law.

Apart from the compulsory gymnastics, anyone could do voluntary work in the gym under the supervision of the gym master to see you did not come to harm, and when school finished at a quarter to four each day, the gym would be kept open as long as it was needed, and one certainly made full use of this to get fit, improve your physique and learn other sports.

I do not think I was a very good gymnast as such, but I was certainly quite good with the dumbbells and the

Indian clubs. In fact later in my school days I was captain of the Indian club team which gave exhibitions, especially on Governors' Day once a year. However, boxing seemed to be a must to protect yourself, as well as a bit of sport, and so we were taught that, and in fact I became the school champion at my weight eventually. Though finally, as a matter of interest, I had to fight my brother, Bill, in the final and he beat me one year.

Fencing was also well taught and again I enjoyed this, but we only did foil and the epée. This led up to higher standards, against other schools, and eventually I became the school champion at both foil and fencing.

Rugby Football

The whole of the two winter terms was taken up with rugby football. It was not actually compulsory, but you had to be a bit of a weakling not to do it. I enjoyed this game and I must remind you at this stage that it was the end of the First World War as regards timing, and post-war, when the masters were mostly still either away in the Services or convalescing, and the school was run by older masters who had come back to hold the fort. Certainly there were no proper organized games and I can remember that many of us clubbed together and arranged our own games, even if it was not a full size. In fact a lot of us in the north area of London used to arrange to play on Hampstead

Heath on a weekend amongst ourselves or with anyone else whom we could get to join us, because we enjoyed the game so much.

When I finished school at Christmas 1923, I had just turned 19 years old (and still had not passed my London matriculation exam.) so I got in touch with the Old Merchant Taylors' and persuaded them that I would like to play rugby football for them for the remainder of that season, and in fact I did, and for several seasons even after I had become a medical student, but only then when there were no matches at St. Thomas' Hospital.

When I was allowed to start at the Medical School at St. Thomas' Hospital in March 1924, I was promptly enlisted to play in the 1st XV, which was a much advanced form of rugger with grown up people. In those days London Medical Schools rugger teams were playing first class rugby football and we had regular fixtures with all the good clubs, such as Bath, Northampton, Leicester, Blackheath, Rosslyn Park, you name it, and while some medical schools like Guys and St. Mary's were better than others, principally because they had scholarships for sporting types, the football was good fun, although some injuries were sustained occasionally.

I continued to play this type of football until I was qualified and then we had a stroke of luck because a particular friend of mine called Bob Williams, who was at Merchant Taylors' as well as at St. Thomas' with me, and who lived at Harpenden, Hertfordshire, and I were the only two people doing our midwifery together. In those days, medical students took priority over the nursing staff as regards training in this form of medicine, and of course we had to have time off as there weren't any other medical students and the nurses took over. They were delighted to do so because they got more experience. Another factor in our favour was that the President of St. Thomas' Rugby Old Boys was a Mr. James Wyatt, FRCS, who was also a gynaecologist and had been at Merchant Taylors' School himself. So we were regarded with some favour and encouraged to keep our football going in spite of the medical training we were undergoing, and this paid off and we really enjoyed ourselves.

After qualifying, it was more difficult to turn out because you had jobs to do, and hours of duty included night work and weekend work. We managed to continue in one form or another, but of course you weren't so fit and you weren't so skilled. Eventually I was promoted to be Captain of the 2nd XV. I liked this because not only did I have my sport to play, but I could keep an eye on the up and coming people who would eventually play in the 1st team. However, finally, when I was a registrar, which meant I was living out, - and in fact I was married by that time, and was still captain of the 2nd XV - I found my left index finger was broken after a match. I don't think this actually occurred during the match but when I fell over in the washrooms and swimming pool area after the match, and I fell on my hand. The result of course was that I had it X-rayed first thing on the Monday morning, and it was confirmed that it was a break and I had to have a little plaster cast, which meant that I could not operate. My chief, Mr. Cyril Nitch, FRCS, one of the consultant surgeons at St. Thomas' Hospital, was far from pleased and persuaded me that in my interests as well as his, I should give up this rough game, and so it had to happen, and that was the end of my rugger career in peace time.

However, when the Second World War started and as a territorial medical officer and officer in charge of the Surgical Division of the 21st General Hospital, Territorial Army, we found ourselves in France with the British Expeditionary Force, and between January and May 1940 before Hitler attacked, we played a lot of rugger matches in a combined medical team, against all comers such as travelling RAF teams, and this we thoroughly enjoyed as well. This particular team, in the Boulogne sub-area as it was called, consisted of a lot of rugby international players including the celebrated Bill Tucker and Lindsay Lewis from Cambridge. I, still as full back, was one of the also-rans as far as skill and technique were concerned. Of course all this came to an end as soon as the hot war started on 10th May 1940, and that really was the end of my rugby career.

However there are two items during this rugger period which stand out in my mind. The first was the fact that before we went to France at about Christmas time 1939, the local Territorial units in Eastbourne raised a rugger side to play the Eastbourne team, and I am pleased to say that I again was asked to play as full back, and not only did we win the match, but I scored my only try from the full back position. The second thing which stands out was that, apart from the broken finger I mentioned earlier, the only other injury I can remember was being concussed. I was the captain of the 'A' XV at St. Thomas' Hospital playing the Hon Artillery Company at our own ground at Chiswick. This was a very good match, and I forget the result, but some time during the first half I do remember going down hard on the ball to prevent it being kicked over our goal line for a try. The next thing I remember is waking up on the touch line covered in people's overcoats to keep me warm, and it was some time after that before I really became conscious enough to get up and return to the field of play. It so happened that in this match I was the only medically qualified member, the others all being students, and as is usual amongst medical teams, nobody pays the slightest attention to anybody being damaged. They just get on with the game and hope somebody else will take over the medical treatment. Well I got up and ran on to the field from the end from which I had left it and tried to field the ball, but I was promptly given off-side by the referee because, in the meanwhile they had had half-time and had reversed ends, and I ran on on the side of the opponents, and committed a good faux-pas. Anyway we finished the game and we entertained our guests in the club house with ginger beer, shandy and tea. At that time I had a motor bike, and old AJS 2¾ horsepower. As I was off at the weekend I had arranged to stay with my parents in Bronsbury Park for a little off duty time, and so I rode home rather shakily and spent the weekend with them, being rather sick at times. The reason I went home, and did not return to the hospital to see about getting some treatment for my concussion, was the fact that a few weeks previously one of my best friends had been concussed and he went back to St. Thomas' to report for duty and was promptly put in a dark, small room off the main ward for a fortnight to recover, and I didn't see myself following suit. I merely reported for duty on the Monday morning as if nothing had happened and as far as I know, I had not suffered any ill effects.

Cricket

This started in Queens Park in a small way as a small boy and continued in the garden at all ages, wrecking the wood of the fence and the greenhouse frequently.
However at school, it was more or less compulsory in the summer, and while there were nets to practise in Charterhouse Square after school hours, no cricket was actually played there. As I said before, we had to

go down to Bellingham twice a week or to some other ground if you were playing in a team. I must say I thoroughly enjoyed my cricket. I think it is a good sport and from the young age of eleven, I found that skill and rhythm which developed as I grew older. I could bowl fairly well and fairly fast. I even took a turn at wicket-keeping. I wasn't a bad bat and enjoyed batting, and I even enjoyed fielding. However I didn't rise to the giddy heights of my middle brother, Bill, who was certainly better than I was and got his colours in the 1st XI, while I got as far as colours in the 2nd XI. When school finished I played a little in the holidays for scratch sides around the Bronsbury Park area and still enjoyed it. But it was no good taking it up at medical school because firstly I didn't think I was good enough, and secondly because it took up a great deal of time - in other words a whole day must be spent for a match. So basically I didn't play any more cricket once I got to medical school.

Shooting

Whether you are in the Officers Training Corps or not, an alternative to playing cricket in the summer was to shoot with the straightforward army rifle, with .303 bullets. However there was a miniature range in the school grounds and one could practise there regularly. In fact we had to do this as a routine as a part of the OTC training, and I found myself to be what they called in those days a first-class shot. So instead of cricket one year, as l wasn't going very far with the cricket, I decided to do shooting, and this took us down to the ranges at Raynham in Essex and Bisley, of course, for the annual competition. It is a very slow sport. Hours are spent in sighting before you pull the trigger, and as I say, I did it for one season to see what it was like, but although I didn't do badly, I was bored by it, and didn't do it again. Although I found that later in life in the Territorials my eye was just as good and when we did our training on the ranges at Eastbourne and other places, I managed to get good scores.

Swimming

While I used to enjoy going to the baths as a young boy, I found I could not swim though, nothing daunted, I used to dive off the sides and even off the board at the deep end. But nothing could induce me to swim, and I had to make sure I got to the side before I sank. We had quite a number of swimming baths round the home area. The indoor baths were in Finchley Road and they were first class, and I was easily able to get to those because my journey to school on the Metropolitan passed Finchley Road if I went on that route and I merely got out and went for a swim on the way home. In the summer time there were two open-air baths, one in Gladstone Park, Willesden Green, Cricklewood, and the other in a big park near Willesden Junction station. At weekends when not doing anything else, and during the holidays, I with friends from the neighbourhood used to spend perhaps the whole day there, taking our lunch. Finally one day for no reason at all, I found I wasn't sinking and from that day on I moved ahead.

At school there was nothing very good about school swimming. We didn't have baths and we had to go to some rather dingy baths in the City Road area, where we used to go to practice to try to get into the school team, which I did. Also there at those baths, we used to practise life saving with a big, very life-like dummy and at these baths the water was so dark you couldn't see the bottom, so you were told to shut your eyes and they threw the dummy in and you jolly well had to find it. You couldn't see it. Anyway I managed to pass that all right and got my life-saving certificate. The highlights of course were the public school swimming sports at the Bath Club in Dover Street, I think it was. It was fun going there but we had one member of our school who was very good and I was the next best but not in the same class in my opinion. While we enjoyed the experience of swimming against other teams, we didn't do very well.

I continued swimming all my life when the occasion arose, especially since going to Eastbourne, and before the war there used to be a club, mostly of doctors, who used to bathe off the pier before breakfast most of the year round. I must say that sometimes it was jolly cold, but it was a good social gathering. We all knew each other and apart from getting cold, we enjoyed it. During the war the pier was disconnected from the mainland in case of invasion and the cabins disappeared and this club did not re-start after the war.

Again, pre-war in Eastbourne, you weren't allowed to bathe off the beach and if they caught you, they charged you tuppence. This means to say that we did and we had spies out to see whether the collector was coming round. But as the family grew we acquired a tent which you arranged either to bring with you every day and put it up yourself, or store it in the Wish Tower and again either put it up yourself or have it put up for you for a fee. You weren't supposed to share with anyone else but of course everybody did including us and this kept down the cost. This was rather fun, and when you got a good summer a lot of swimming was carried out.

Post-war in the summer of 1945 we started going down in our bathing wraps and there weren't any tents about, and they started coming round trying to charge us tuppence a time. I amongst others put my foot down and said that we were not going to pay this any more, gave our name and address, and then the Town Council scrapped the whole thing. So from then on we just went down, took the car, parked it, had a bathe and then back to the car, mostly wet. We changed at home, had lunch and so on. During the last two or three years we have had a beach hut which is a nice luxury and you can change and sit there on a deck chair and enjoy yourself. So at 88+ we still swim (1993).

Tennis

At school there was no squash in those days and there was no tennis. If you were thought to be a tennis player, you were regarded as a cissy and lost a lot of marks in everybody's estimation. So I didn't start tennis until I was about fifteen, and that was only because my mother belonged to a club, at which she played in the match team, and she was quite a good player herself, this being a grass court club. I was taken along as a young schoolboy and asked to do a bit of practising to see how I got on. And I found I had a bit of an aptitude for it so I continued with it. When I was about 17 or 18 we changed to a bigger club near Willesden Green called Southhampstead Cricket Club which had as a separate item nine grass courts in a row on one side of the field, and a separate clubhouse and a separate committee. In those days, I was introduced by my parents and I had to turn up in long white trousers and blazer and a tie, of all things. Everybody wore ties on the men's side, and the men wore straw hats and so on. But it was a good club. My tennis improved and I continued there until I finally left to come to Eastbourne in 1935. Before leaving in my later years at the club I was the singles champion for two or three years.

On coming to Eastbourne, one of my partners, called

Dr. Churcher, had a grass tennis court and I was persuaded to join the prominent Eastbourne Grass Court Club called 'The Upperton Club' in Gildredge Park for the summer season. That was also a nine grass-court club, with its own clubhouse and groundsman. I enjoyed that very much. There was a good mixed crowd and we played lots of matches and there again, by the time war started in 1939, I was the singles champion.

Of course there was no tennis during the war, except at one camp, Cosel, that I visited. They had made themselves a hard court of sorts and got some racquets from the International Red Cross and a few balls, and I was invited to have a bash, which was rather fun although under prison conditions.

After the war I came back to Eastbourne and with the president, who was an old Cambridge tennis blue, with a title, myself and another committee member, a solicitor, we went to the Town Council who had acquired Gildredge Park and they said no more tennis, kindly remove your two clubhouses and all your equipment, netting and so on. And that was that.

So I joined Devonshire Park, which is a beautiful park with marvellous grass, and for many years after the war, it really was a delight to play there because there was so much ground that they could put six or eight courts in a row, and there was room for three rows, and except for big tournaments they only had one row at a time, so the grass never got worn and always had two months or more to recover before it was re-used. However, this being Corporation owned, you didn't have much say in what went on. It was only your own club on paper. We were granted the use of a pavilion in which we could sit, have tea and make tea, provided they didn't want it for some other purpose, and then we were thrown out. Certain major tournaments were played during the year, like the County Championships, which was doubles, and during that time the whole three rows of courts were used and it took up five days of the week and there wasn't any play for ordinary club members.

As the years went by, the Corporation fixed up more and more big tournaments, professional tournaments, you name it, and the ground became more and more used by outsiders for the benefit of the town's popularity, and the local club members were given a very back seat. In fact sometimes you couldn't even get a court to play on, so eventually I gave that up. But I enjoyed my years because I played in the 1st match team and eventually when I got a bit older I was captain of the 2nd match team and kept an eye on the up and coming youngsters, who could then proceed to the 1st team.

The disadvantages of this club were two-fold. Firstly there were no hard courts and no winter tennis. This is not strictly true because there were some hard courts but they were not allowed to form a club there and they were merely for hire for anyone who wanted one. The second thing was that the season ended early because in those days they had a croquet championship in September and so we had to finish tennis by the end of August so that they could get the ground ready for the croquet tournament. That I think has now disappeared but they still have so many tournaments going on later in the year that the ground shuts early to ordinary club members.

Of course all this time, wherever I lived in Eastbourne, I had a grass tennis court of my own. We had lots of fun and you could practise and bring your friends in and that still continues to this day. But when I left Devonshire Park tennis club for the reasons I have already mentioned, I joined the Upperton Tennis Club in Gildredge Park, which was recently formed on the site of the original grass courts of the old pre-war Upperton Club. This only happened because there was a splendid club in Kings Drive, Eastbourne, which was privately owned and in those days was the only club, being privately owned, where you could play before 2 o'clock on a Sunday. The Corporation was very strict about this, so that at this particular club, apart from being a nice club, you could play on a Sunday morning, for what is the use of starting tennis at 2 o'clock in mid-winter when it gets dark about 3 o'clock. Anyway, eventually the owners of this private club, the Kings Drive Tennis Club, sold the whole ground for a building site, and somehow the Corporation relented and allowed people to put up three hard courts, as I say, in Gildredge Park on the site of the old Upperton Club. So this club I joined and still play there, and am actually the President.

I might add that when we came back from the Second World War, and they wouldn't let us play any more, the remains of the pre-war Committee presented me with the Singles Challenge Cup because although it was played in 1940 after I had become a prisoner of war, the chap who won it that year has never been heard of since. I have still got it on my shelf, a splendid memento.

Photo of Tom, at age 92, taken from the British LTA's magazine ACE, edition of November 1997.

Photos taken at the time of a photo-op, organized by **ACE** magazine, of Tom Wilson (*aged 94*) hitting with Tom Lester (*aged 4*) for an article published in the October 1998 edition.

The Two Toms

(Editor's notes :

1 - after the death of Tom Wilson, the family donated that Singles Challenge Cup trophy to the Gildredge Park Tennis Club, to be used as they saw fit – possibly for something like ' the most promising or improved young player'. In essence, it was being returned to its original club by its last known winner, after a period of 61 years!)

2 – in 1997, ACE magazine, the official magazine for the British LTA, decided to do an article, titled "Golden Oldies", to support the idea that tennis is not just a game for the young and for professionals, but is a game for anyone and for life. To this end, they tried to "locate some of the oldest active tennis players in Britain to ask them what keeps them going".

The article came out in the November 1997 issue of ACE, and it started by saying that "At 92, Tom Wilson is the oldest active player ACE could find", with accompanying splendid photographs, and a few words stemming from an interview.

A note of interest to me personally was that the photograph showed him dressed as usual in his white pants, shirt, and sweater, and on the sweater was sewn the badge of the Monkland Tennis Club, of Montreal, Canada – my own Club! Whenever my father came to visit me in Montreal, I enrolled him as a temporary member of the Club so that he would always feel that he could go there at any time, without waiting to be taken there.

3 – As a follow-up to the 1997 article, in 1998, the staff at ACE asked if my father would agree to participate in a photo-op for a later article in which they had my father, just less than 94, hitting with a youngster of just-turned 4, whom ACE brought down from Peterborough, with his parents. The youngster (Tom Lester) had started playing at age 3, and had shown an extraordinary talent for hitting a tennis ball, worthy of grooming for the future.

They played on the grass courts at the Devonshire Park, in Eastbourne, lately the site of the Ladies pre-Wimbledon tennis tournament. Unfortunately, although the action took place in July, the weather was appalling, with rain, which did not make for easy tennis for young or old!

The article came out in the October 1998 issue of ACE, and was titled "The Two Toms", since they were in fact both called Tom. Apparently they enjoyed each other's company and got on well.

Squash

I first started to play this game when I was a registrar at St. Thomas' Hospital at the time I broke my finger playing rugger. It so happened that a very short time before this event, the students' club at St. Thomas' had built, as part of the club, two squash courts, changing rooms and showers, and so on. I didn't find any difficulty in finding opponents with the large student population, and I thoroughly enjoyed these games.

When I moved to Eastbourne in 1935, I found two very nice squash courts as part of Devonshire Park, and so I joined the club and continued playing. It is a very good game to play when you are working because you can get a large amount of exercise in a very short space of time and in a very small area of space. It is a fast game and you have to have a good eye. When you are working fairly hard, you can arrange a match to suit your work timetable, and help to keep fit, because there is no doubt in my case that if you keep fit you do better work, and can work longer hours without suffering from fatigue. After the war, I re-joined the club until the time came when I could not get anybody to play against because you must play somebody about your own vintage and about your own level of skill. Otherwise if you are not as skilled as your opponent by a long chalk, you don't enjoy it and equally if you are much better than your opponent. Also if you try to play somebody very much younger and even better, who is more active than you are, you kill yourself. So eventually I had to stop playing because the people with whom I was used to playing against became either disabled or had heart attacks, and that was the end of my squash.

Badminton

This is another good game which I played in a casual manner in London, merely joining other people to make up a set, and I did not take it very seriously, except it was another game to play. When I moved to Eastbourne, I found there were a number of small, private clubs, who all used the Devonshire Park Baths which were closed in the winter and converted into badminton courts. I joined one run by another surgeon's wife, a Mrs Turner, with a limited membership of about 30 people. We hired a court twice a week for the evening and fortunately the whole group never turned up all together, because the more people who turned up the longer you had to sit out between sets, and if you had a short set because you won or lost easily, sometimes you had a long wait. As there was no heating in the baths it was very cold. In fact I finally gave up this game some time after the war because I used to get too cold in evenings late

late evenings and I don't think it did me any good from my work point of view.

Hockey

I didn't play hockey until wartime. At that time I was a prisoner of war and found myself in a large camp called Stalag VIII B, later renamed or renumbered 344 in Silesia, which was a camp holding 20,000. Some prisoners had made a hockey pitch and sticks were available, having been sent to the camp through the International Red Cross. There were a lot of Indians in this camp who played hockey very well and mostly in bare feet. As a means of getting some exercise I asked if I could join in, and eventually became fairly proficient on this hard, dried mud pitch, and in fact I represented the Lazarette (Hospital) team as an outside left forward. Not an ideal position for a right-hander as you have to pass the ball smartly from left to right which is an unnatural thing to do.

When I got back to Eastbourne and re-started hospital work, I found they had been running a mixed-gender Hospital hockey side and I offered my services and was invited to play in several matches against other teams in the area. I found this game much rougher than in prisoner-of-war life amongst men only, and on one occasion I split my hand and had to be careful in my surgical work. But what finally made me give up was when I slipped on a muddy pitch and cut my knee right across the kneecap so badly that I had to leave the field. I took myself to St. Mary's Hospital where the medical superintendent, Dr Ian Brown, took pity on me, admitted me to the theatre and sewed me up. Needless to say, this did not heal smoothly and became infected, and that leads me to another little story, because I was the commanding officer at that time of a Territorial medical unit in Eastbourne and after this knee was cut, I had to be present at a social function in mess dress, which you will remember consisted of very tight trousers. I barely got them over my knee dressing and it was very uncomfortable. However I lasted the evening and when I got home I had to get help from the family to take off my clothes, and this was the first time they had known about the accident as I kept it very quiet when continuing with my work. That I am afraid to say was the end of my hockey.

Skiing

I first started this in 1930. At that time I, with seven others, was a casualty officer at St. Thomas' Hospital, and after six months in that appointment, we had a fortnight's holiday. This was followed by a second six months either as a house physician or a house surgeon, and I was to be a house surgeon. This fortnight's break occurred in January and February and we all said 'what the blazes can we do in a fortnight in London at this time of the year when it is cold and miserable?'

One of my colleagues said he had skied before and why didn't we all go skiing, and that is what happened. One of the eight did all the arranging and we paid our money over, and set off to Switzerland. We had to do this skiing holiday in Switzerland as cheaply as possible because none of us was well off, and in fact most of us were decidedly poor, as the appointments at a London teaching hospital were unpaid, although you got board and lodging, and so you had to rely on your own private means or get your parents to help you out where necessary.

So we elected to go the cheap route - from Victoria by train to Newhaven, then by boat to Dieppe, followed by another train to Paris, which we reached in the early evening and had a leisurely dinner in a good restaurant, after which we proceeded to the second station and took the train to Switzerland, travelling overnight. This meant sitting up in a compartment and dozing off as best you could, once the conversation had dried up. We arrived at Interlaken after daylight, where we had to change trains to take the mountain railway up to Wengen, which was our destination. This was all new to all of us except the one who had been before and who had arranged the holiday, and so it was a thrill to see the mountains and the scenery, with snow, and trying to get some food at wayside stations using our best French or German as necessary. We disembarked at Wengen, I don't know what time now, but probably before lunch. We must have been shown to our rooms and told what the procedures were, times of meals, and so on. The next thing was to get out into the village and get hold of some ski equipment for hire.

Wengen is a delightful village, not too big, 3,000 feet up, and there are no cars. There is a road up but it is not used in the winter and everything is done either with horses, as it was in those days, or on your flat feet or skis. In the centre of the village are an ice-skating rink and a curling rink, and just beyond that is a large area for beginners with a little fairly steep slope on one side going down to a flattish area at the bottom at village street level. I thought it was the most delightful place that I had ever been to, and we had a marvellous fortnight.

Tom in Wengen, Switzerland in 1930, with fellow medical students from St. Thomas' Hospital.

We set off after lunch and went to one of the sports shops and got fitted up with skis and ski sticks. We each of course had our own clothing which was quite different in those days from what it is nowadays, as is the ski equipment, boots and the skis themselves. In 1930 my skis clothes consisted of my Territorial Army riding breeches, a pair of walking boots I borrowed from another chap at St Thomas', and puttees. Above the waist we had several thick sweaters, thick shirts, and some form of covering such as a warm jacket which would keep out the snow but would not keep out rain. Then of course we had to have a cap of some sort and if you didn't like the light you had to have a pair of dark glasses. The skis themselves were hickory I think and there were no metal edges, so that the type that you hired had been well used without any decent edge and they were pretty well rounded. They were not fixed to the boot in any way - you merely crammed the toe of your boot into a metal device, rather like they have for roller skating, and the strap was tightened up to keep the toe in position, while there was another strap round the back of your heel with a spring on it, which you hoped would keep you jammed forward into the toecap and wouldn't keep coming out. That was the only control you had, as in those days there were no release bindings, and no safety devices if you fell over and had your ski too tight.

We were shown how to put them on, and then we had to walk up part of the slope and try to put them on without falling down the hill, and eventually, when you did get them on, the one and only skier said 'you point them downhill and hope for the best', and this is basically what we did. There were no ski teachers in those days and you just had to find out how to do it the hard way by watching other people. The one thing you had to learn as quickly as you could was how to stop.

In the early days you did what was a stem position, in other words the front of each ski was pointed at an angle to meet or nearly touch the other ski point, and when you bent your knees and try to press the skis outwards, it acted as a snow plough and that is what it was called - a snow plough position - and if you had strong legs, particularly thigh muscles, you could push against almost anything and come to a halt. And so when going downhill in the early stages you merely pointed them both down with the points near each other and the farther out the back parts were the slower you went. If you were lucky you managed to stop where you wanted to, and try to miss other people, - and if you were unlucky, you fell over. . As you got better, you learned to go down gently with your skis parallel, and you could do a skid one way or the other so that you became parallel with the slope and therefore came to a stop.

About the third day we were there, the railway which went up to Scheidegg, which is at about 6,000 ft, was carried away by an avalanche just outside the village.

It not only carried the railway, but it carried the trees and was a highly dangerous thing to happen, and if you were anywhere near it, it was pretty well certain death. So when we got our ski legs, and thought we would take the train to the next level up and practise coming down through the woods, we could not get a train because they were not working.

This of course did us a lot of good because although we were young and fairly fit, if you had to walk uphill it was quite hard work and your muscles got stronger every day, and when you have got strong muscles you are much less likely to have an accident and do some real damage. Of course walking uphill is not easy - you have to go very gently across a slope and the only way to go steeper is to put on what are called 'skins'. The skins come in pairs, one for each ski. They are about 2-2½ inches wide, made of seal skin, and they are long enough to go from the point of the ski to the back of the ski. There is a canvas strap with a loop which fits over the point of the ski and there is a strap at the back which tightens it up, and while there are others - one in front and one behind your boots - cross-straps to stop it sliding sideways. With these in position you can go up a hill I would think at about 30 degrees without any slipping backwards. Mark you, it is tiring and it takes about an hour to do 1,000 ft. So we walked for about an hour one day up the railway track, and round the avalanche a track had been made for us so we could get through the avalanche, and we then stopped and had a rest.

After about another hour's walk, you come to what was a little halt on the railway and it is called The Bumps. This is because there is a big open space free of trees which is very undulating and with a sharp slope on the left side down to the ravine, hence the name Bumps, because as you go down you really do go up and down over these bumps. There is quite a good place for practising more skiing when you got past the beginners' stage because you have to find your way and do some turning from left to right, mostly to the right. When you get to the end of this large expanse of open, bumpy snowfield, the track then enters the trees and continues through the trees from there on down back into Wengen, but there is only one way to enter these trees by the track and you have to judge it rather well. If you go too far down to the left you have to climb back up again, but if you get it right, you enter a fairly narrow space and almost immediately there is a very sharp 180 degree turn to the left. You can imagine if you miss this you go up into the trees and are likely to do yourself a bit of damage. But it also takes a bit of courage and skill and it really is quite a sharp bend on a little bit of a slope, and if you are going at a reasonable speed and don't do it right, you can twist your knees, and hence this particular spot is known as Slip Cartilage Corner.

From then on down to Wengen is a nice run through wood paths, but these I never liked because they tended to get into ruts and if you got into ruts like tramlines you couldn't get out again, and it is not at all easy to stop. One eventually gets down into the outskirts of Wengen and here you have to stop, take off your skis and walk uphill under the railway archway and back into the top end of the village. As you get stronger and better, in our case we had to walk to the top at Scheidegg where again it is a nice run down, mostly on formed tracks until you get to a little station called Wengen-Alp where there is a small hotel. This is a good stopping point in either direction because they served good snacks and drinks and you can have a sit down and rest in the sunshine.

In Wengen-Alp, as a matter of interest, there is a plaque on the wall issued by the British Government thanking them for all the help they gave to escaped British prisoners-of-war who had got into Switzerland somehow. Of course, most of them couldn't get out again, as it was a neutral country, and a lot of them stayed there for the rest of the war. And this plaque thanks the local people and the hotel in particular for all the help they gave to those prisoners-of-war.

You continue down the track until you get to the Bumps and then you have the course which I described before.

When we got fitter and stronger, we were able to get as far as Scheidegg by lunchtime, where we had our packed lunch and possibly a drink, and then set off down the other side towards Grindelwald. This again is a lovely run, going first of all through open fields and later on coming to the trees.

The first time we did this, it took us all day to get to Grindelwald , and as we had to climb up back to Scheidegg and ski back home to Wengen, we knew we would never make it, so we chickened out and took the train round to Interlaken and then changed into the mountain one back up to Wengen, and we thought we well deserved our dinner that evening.

As time went on we got stronger and fitter and eventually we managed to walk up to Scheidegg, ski down the other side, have some refreshments and walk most of the way back to Scheidegg and ski home to Wengen.

And those are really the highlights of our holiday.

If you wanted to go on a tour when you got up to Scheidegg, you had to put on your skins and climb up either the summer or winter pass to a mountain called Lauberhorn. This again was a delightful journey and when the trains were working, you could get up to Scheidegg quickly and set about this trip up the Lauberhorn, and then ski back, either to Scheidegg or by a circular route to more or less the half-way station on the Wengen railway down to Wengen-Alp, and so home. And the same applied on the Grindelwald side. There were excursions to be made there on the other side of Grindelwald and if you had the energy and the time and the weather was right, the fact that the railways were working meant that you could go much further afield and enjoy the scenery as well.

In addition to the skiing of course there was a social life. You met people at the various halts, such as Wengen-Alp and Scheidegg and you sat and talked to them while you ate your lunch or tea, whichever time of day it was, and then you got back to your hotel in the evening in time to have some tea if you felt like it, and then there was time for a leisurely bath and change in those days into dinner jackets every evening, after which there was what is now known as the après-ski where you went to the dance floor hoping to get some dancing. We being six bachelors managed to get some dancing in and I don't remember anything about the girls with whom we danced. By the time you had had an evening's entertainment, dancing and socializing, you didn't get to bed very early, but when you are young you can manage these things without any trouble and think nothing of it.

As well as the skiing, there were of course ice rinks and the curling rinks. We none of us had time to try curling, but I for one hired some skates and did a bit of skating, because I had done this in Britain in places like Holland Park in the old days.

The time came when our holiday came to an end and

we had to take the train back to Interlaken and from there through to Basle or somewhere like that to catch the main railway back to Paris, then Dieppe, across the sea to Newhaven and back to Victoria. I believe the next day we had to report for duty, and commenced our second six months, in my case as a house surgeon to Mr. Max Page and Mr. Robinson.

Now of course that wasn't the end of the skiing life, as the bug had got me as they say, and I was lucky in that my only real friend in my home area was a man of similar age called Jack Andrews, the son of Arthur Andrews and Mrs Andrews who lived at 232 Willesden Lane. He and I had similar interests in life, both in tennis, golf and skiing, and I must say in each sport I think he was certainly better than I was.

As a matter of interest he was at Cambridge, at Gonville and Caius College, and he was a first class rifle shot and in fact represented England in international events while still a student at Cambridge, for which he got a half blue. I can also say that in one year he should have won the Kings Cup at Bisley but the final 1,000 yards was shot in a gale and he had one shot to go and he only had to hit the target to win, but for some unexplained reason he hit the neighbouring target and so he failed to score, and was beaten by a point by the runner-up, who was a lady called Miss Foster. Such is shooting and all the hazards that go with it.

As Jack and I got on very well in most things, although he went to St. Paul's School while I went to Merchants Taylors', we met regularly in our home area and we decided that we would like to go skiing together, and in fact we did this twice at Wengen before the 2nd World War started. It could have been three times even, but we certainly didn't do it every year owing either to my employment or his. These were delightful skiing years because, as I said, he was certainly better than I was, he could ski more often, he was delightful company and we got better and better every year, although you can't get terribly good if you only have a fortnight a year or not even every year. But it is a wonderful holiday, free from what I call civilization - no cars and a leisurely life apart from physical exercise. We stayed each time at a hotel called the Belvedere, which was a bigger hotel than the Silverhorn I think, farther up the village, but it had a very good menu, good rooms with views over the valley and the railway, and a very good dance floor and band. We were both reasonably good dancers and enjoyed going down to the dance hall in the evening after dinner and dancing with whichever girl or lady who happened to be available, without making any permanent friendships.

Then came the war and I was not one of those who were lucky enough to get to an area where in slack times skiing was available. So I had to wait until the war was ended.

It so happened that I was put in command of a medical territorial unit in Eastbourne and my quartermaster on the permanent staff, looking through the ACI (Army Council Instruction) which appeared regularly, pointed out to me that there was a note from the Army Ski Association, talking about its existence, its headquarters in London in Belgrave Square, and its aims and objects. So the next time I went to London for a meeting of surgeons, I went to this office and was introduced to a Col Redhead, DSO. I had a tie at the time which led him to believe I was a gold standard skier of British standards gold, but when I was able to disabuse him on this, he took far less interest in me, he himself being a gold standard and representing Britain in skiing events.

However, he put me in touch with the organization. I paid my entrance fee for which I then received the programme of winter sports events run by the Army Ski Association. From then on I took my holidays regularly in Switzerland almost every year for the rest of my skiing life through the service organizations.

I must add here that apart from the Army Winter Sports Association there was also the Navy, and the Air Force, and a fourth which was called the Combined Winter Sports Association. I mention this now because the latter Association, from its foundation, had as its secretary a lady whose name then was Valerie Storey, and she ran this association with a small team. The Committee work was of course chaired by Admirals, Generals or Field-Marshals, or Air Vice-Marshals, depending on which service was in command by rotation.

As my family did not ski, being on the young side after the War, and my particular friend Jack Andrews had been killed at Derna in North Africa in the Second World War, I had to either find somebody I could take a holiday with, or just go solo, and join one of the winter sports parties where of course you got to know a large number of people in a short time. For a time I went on my own to St. Moritz, staying in the early days at the Hotel Albana which is in the centre of the town. The food was not particularly good but it was a very convenient location. You met a large number of service people and their families and a most enjoyable fortnight was had by everybody, whether at skiing or après-ski.

Some time later there was an appointment made at the Chaseley Home for Disabled Ex-Servicemen for Group Captain Stradling, late of the RAF, who was a keen skier. Although he was a little bit older than I was, we got on well together at our work at Chaseley and decided to take a holiday together. We were skiing well and decided to visit Wengen under the Army ski scheme. This was a great success and he knew lots of people there who went there regularly and I was persuaded to join the local British club called the Downhill Only Club. We did this several years running until he himself thought that his skiing days were over, so I had to look around again.

Another of my friends was an orthopaedic surgeon named Eric Bintcliffe, who worked at Bexhill, Hastings, and Tunbridge Well. He was an expert skier, much better than I could ever be, having learned in the north of Italy as part of his career in the Army during the war. He also had two young sons who had started to ski and were quite good and we made quite a nice little foursome. The four of us went fairly regularly to St. Moritz and stayed at the hotel half way down the hill to the St. Moritzbad, the Belvue Hotel.

This was a nice family hotel, filled mostly by service people, the only snag being you either had to walk up the hill to the station in the morning, or if you were lucky to get a bus. We had some splendid years together until finally Eric Bintcliffe developed cancer and died relatively young. By that time his sons were more or less grown up and they were first class skiers in every way. Another interesting point about Eric Bintcliffe was that one year I decided to go to Zermatt under the scheme run by the RAF Association. This only occurred because several things happened which stopped me going to St. Moritz that year and in fact my booking into Zermatt was the third effort to get a holiday.

Zermatt was a delightful place - another resort where there are no cars and so different from Wengen that it made a totally different kind of holiday. I soon got to know other members in the holiday hotel and we had some expert skiing. In those days, which was 1956, there wasn't the amount of skiing available that there is now at Zermatt and there is really only the mountain called Gornergrat with a railway up to it which gave you good skiing, but the runs were limited. All the time you had the marvellous view of the mountain opposite, called the Matterhorn, but there was no skiing available in that area. Most days we went around with a guide and there was a particular half a dozen of us who used this guide.

Until one day we were coming down from the Gornergrat and I was the sweeper, or tail-end Charlie, when coming round the mountain clockwise on a fairly narrow path I came across a woman who was obviously not a very good skier and she blocked the path. I don't know how my friends managed to pass but perhaps it was a bit wider when they met her. I seemed to have two alternatives - one to crash her and sit down and possibly hurt both of us, and the other to go over the left hand edge onto soft snow and try and get round her. There wasn't much time to think and I could not slow down on this narrow pass so I took the option of going round her and the next thing I knew was an almighty noise of splintering skis, and presumably my leg as well, and I found myself upside down in the soft snow with a broken leg on the right side. The lady was quite oblivious to this and she went on, and I imagine she caught up with my friends who eventually walked back to find out what had happened to me. I myself was in a fair amount of discomfort and found that my right leg was back to front. I managed to get the skis off somehow and just had to sit pretty.

My friends covered me up with all the spare bits of clothing they had and somebody must have sent for the first aid team which was called the blood wagon. The team and the wagon had to take the train up to the top and ski down and find me, which they eventually did. I must say that in my medical capacity I thought they were first class and they soon had me under sedation with some pain-killing pills, and they worked very fast. They covered me up to keep me warmer and put a balloon type of splint on my leg which they blew up to stop it being jolted around, strapped the legs together, hoisted me on the blood wagon and set off down back to Zermatt with one chap in the front holding the two handles of the sledge and one behind with a rope attached to the back of the sledge to make sure it didn't overrun the chap in front, and to help to steer it. A long way to go and I must say it was very bumpy and exhilarating, but I got colder and colder and I could not stop my teeth chattering. As it was a long way from home, they stopped at a point on the railway line and the railway carriages were made available, and that was a bit warmer down to the station at Zermatt. From there I was taken straight to the clinic and seen by the surgeon in charge.

He was a most able man and saw to my comfort, undid all the splints carefully and my clothes were split up, and X-rays were taken. When I saw the X-rays myself I was absolutely shattered because I had what they call a comminuted, complicated and open fracture of the tibia and fibula on the right side. The pieces in between the top and bottom halves of the tibia seemed to be so numerous and small that I couldn't imagine anybody putting them together again. I then decided that I wanted to get home rather than stay in Zermatt because I knew they would probably put me to bed in splints or traction and I would be there for months. When the surgeon heard what I had to say he was very cooperative and plastered me up, dressed the open wound, and gave me an antibiotic injection which I think must have been streptomycin, and put me to bed for the night because the last train had already left Zermatt.

Next morning the surgeon came to see me and made sure I was as comfortable as possible, and gave me some pain-killing injections, and I was dressed up and taken to the train on a magnificent sledge with horn shaped handles, with an Alpine guide. You couldn't travel in the train itself you had to travel in the guards' van and it was jolly cold. I forget how you get to Geneva from Zermatt now. It was guards' van all the way until we got to Geneva, when I was handed over to the British Airline personnel and put on a plane back to Heathrow.

I must add that the night before setting off for home, I managed to telephone my wife, Olive, in Eastbourne to tell her what was happening and asked her if she could get hold of the Eastbourne orthopaedic surgeon, a friend of mine called Mr. Jenkins, and arrange a bed for me at the Princess Alice Hospital, where the orthopaedic centre was situated in those days.

The flight in the plane was comfortable. They had taken out two rows of seats and fixed in some sort of plinth which I imagine they could strap a coffin to as well. Instead of which they strapped my stretcher. The airline staff were very good and at one stage they gave me an injection in the arm to ease my discomfort, which it did, but I must confess that it was given very shallowly under the skin and eventually the whole area became dead and sloughed off, leaving an ulcer which took a long time to heal, the same as the paraplegics get.

On arrival at Heathrow, to my surprise I was met by my friend Eric Bintcliffe with an ambulance, and he travelled with me back to Eastbourne, and Princess Alice Hospital, by then the time being late in the day, where they had a bed ready for me. I don't remember much else but I was told afterwards that I was taken to the theatre as soon as possible after arriving there, and Mr. Jenkins and Eric Bintcliffe, with Dr Kent as anaesthetist, spent a large part of the night putting my leg together, for which I was eternally grateful. I woke up next morning in a little side room and found my leg in plaster, from the toes to the groin, and when Mr. Jenkins later came to talk to me, and showed me the X-rays, somehow they had managed to put a plate in to hold the top and the bottom of the tibia in alignment and the bits in between were put in position and some screws put in to some of the bigger ones as well. How they managed this I don't really know. It must have been a great bit of surgery.

After a few days I was transferred to the Esperance Nursing Home, which was run by the nuns, where I had a comfortable room and was jolly well looked after. I will not write a lot about my injuries except to say that I had this plaster on for nine months during which time, at least a lot of the time, I was not able to work. When I thought I was able to work, the South Eastern Regional Hospital Board decided that they would not re-employ me until I was without any plaster. However this didn't stop me doing private operations and seeing private patients. But enough of that.

I thought that would be the end of my skiing but twelve months later I took the family up to Gamages in London to see the Christmas decorations, and Gamages always had a special toy department with model railways, and you name it. It was a thing to see and I used to see it when I was a small boy at Merchant Taylors' School, as it was not far from the school. During that visit to Gamages, where my sister in-law, Enid Hopper, was Mr. Gamage's private secretary, we had a special look round and were treated like VIPs. After a time I left the family with Enid Hopper and took the bus to the Combined Ex-Services Winter Sports' Association which that year, 1956, was located in one of the houses on the edge of Regents' Park. I merely went to see if there was any chance of getting back to Switzerland, preferably to St. Moritz, just to have a holiday, without any real thought of doing any skiing, and to take the family with me. In this I was very lucky because when I got to the office I found another lady in front of me being interviewed by one of the staff, and she couldn't make her mind up what she wanted to do. So while she thought about it they came to me and I told them what I had in mind - to take my wife Olive and the youngster Sandra, who was then about eight years old, and they said I could have the two last places and we managed to fit Sandra in somewhere   So I think I diddled the lady in front of me and accepted these places. I don't know who it was I talked to then but it could well have been my Valerie Storey herself.

I went back to Gamages, had lunch with them and told them what I had been doing and what I had in mind, and they all said I was mad. But it had all been arranged and so in January or February 1957 we went to St Moritz and stayed at a hotel in St Moritzbad called the National. This is a lovely hotel of typical Swiss type which seemed to be entirely made of wood, and the typical Swiss type of architecture. The food was reasonable, the room was comfortable and its only drawback was that it was a long way from the ski station at St Moritzdorf.

There was a bus which ran regularly and if you were lucky you could take it. It was during this trip that I tried myself out again on skis and found that I could manage reasonably well, but I am afraid Sandra didn't take to skiing easily because she went to a class which had a German speaking teacher and they didn't get on well. She finally decided not to proceed with skiing, and hired a toboggan. This of course meant that I had to do some tobogganing with Sandra and I thought it was much more dangerous than skiing, but we enjoyed ourselves, and had a jolly good fortnight.

I well remember one particular skiing party in the earlier days after the war when flying had not become possible and so you still had to travel by train and boat. This holiday was under the Army ski scheme and we decided to go to a place in the north of Italy called Sestrière. The party consisted of me, Leslie Lauste, a surgeon at Brighton, and the director of the Radiotherapy Clinic at Brighton called Desmond Millington and his wife. The lady, whom I had not met before, was a barrister in her own right and had a very high IQ level and seemed to have a great amount of detailed information on almost any subject you liked to think of.

As I said, we still had to go by train and boat and as

most of them lived in Brighton, we decided to go from Newhaven to Dieppe and via Paris. It so happened that I had operated upon the chief engineer of the Channel ferry we were using and he said that if we ever travelled that way to let him know because the captain would like to entertain us on the trip. I might add that this engineer had developed a cancer of his bowel and I was able to relieve him of this cancer and he survived many years afterwards and died from something else.

So we let him know and when we boarded the ship we were expected, were met at the gangway and conducted to our seats in the lounge, but later the captain himself came and talked to us and invited us up to the bridge. He even let us try to navigate or rather should we say steer the ship, and you could tell when you looked at the stern that the regular chap wasn't doing it because the kerfuffle that shows behind the ship in its wake, instead of being nice and straight, was really wobbly and all over the place, which caused great amusement among the ferry crew. After this we were invited to the captain's private quarters and we all had lunch together on the captain, and it was a great occasion. I might add also that on our return journey, it was the same ship and we were received royally, but he did not give us a lunch at that time.

However, to proceed with the holiday, we arrived in Sestrière having got off the train some several hours' distance from the town and we had to complete the journey by bus. When we got there we realized that the hotel was a circular one, like a tower block only circular, and this was quite amusing because the stairway went continually in a spiral fashion from the ground floor to the top, leaving a centre well down which you could look and I suppose fall. All the rooms opened off this spiral staircase and their windows were on the outer wall, so that each room was narrower at the door end than it was at the window end, and I must say it was quite interesting to stay in this sort of room when you weren't skiing, and entertain your friends there.

The hotel was good and comfortable and like any other served quite reasonable meals. The beds were comfortable, with baths and showers adequate, and there were no complaints on that score at all.

The skiing at Sestrière wasn't all that good from the point of view of runs and nice scenery, and the weather wasn't particularly good anyway. Without boasting, I found that I was easily the best of all of us at skiing but that didn't matter because every now and again I joined another group and had a longer and better ski run than I did by staying with our particular bunch, who didn't want to do too much anyway.

The sad thing about this journey was that one day we were all standing together on a little hilltop chatting amicably when the radiotherapy chap just fell over sideways by losing his balance, and in doing so broke his ankle, which is usually a very easy way of breaking an ankle So we gave him first aid and pain-killing pills, got the blood wagon and he was eventually taken to the local clinic and put in plaster. This rather spoiled his holiday as naturally he couldn't ski any more, but he was with us for the rest of the time on the social occasions and for meals. It was at these mealtimes in the evening that I came to realize what a terrific brain his wife had and I just sat there and listened and tried to take it all in.

Eventually of course we made our way home to Britain, as I said by train and boat, and returned to our normal duties in the surgical and radiological world.

There was one sad result of this broken ankle which I didn't find out for a long time, but our friend Millington became a drug addict and unfortunately eventually had to give up his post and retire early. However we kept in touch until, being Australian, he eventually went back to his own country.

There was another nice year when my daughter, Anthea, who was then doing her nursing training at the Nightingale School at St Thomas' Hospital, joined us for a fortnight at St Moritz, together with Eric Bintcliffe and his two boys. Anthea was quite a competent skier and it gave her a jolly good holiday, something quite different from nursing, so she returned refreshed to continue her training. But I think it was during this trip that she had a bit of a strain to one of her knees and I don't think she skied any more after that.

Many years later, when I went on my own to St. Moritz and joined in the general party, I managed to keep in a class run by a splendid fellow called Alfredo, who was himself a very good skier although not as young as we were. He certainly looked after us well and took us on lovely runs and made sure we didn't come to any harm. For those who don't know St. Moritz, there is a great variety of ski runs and some are more difficult than others, but none are what I would call easy. St. Moritz itself is at 6,000 ft level and you can go up by train and cable car to a mountain called Piz Nair which is between 9,000 and 10,000 ft. The first stage from the town and railway station is a relatively straightforward, a short but steep run to the lower level of the ski slopes called Chantarella. There, when you get out of the train, you can walk steadily up a gentle slope to the nursery slopes as they are called, where beginners practise and become fit to the higher runs, so you can't get anywhere without going up by one train and then by walking quite a way to the ski school.

Those who have got past this stage get into another train which winds quite a way round the slopes until it comes to a further level of about 7,500 ft. called

Corviglia. From here you can ski down to St Moritz, or you can take another route down to Celerina and back to St Moritz by road or train. If you want to go higher from Corviglia, you can take the cable car to Piz Nair, and after that if you want to go exploring you have to climb, but from Piz Nair there are some marvellous runs in all directions, some difficult and some less so, but marvellous skiing and marvellous views.

I must add that the south facing slope from Piz Nair top I think has now been banned for skiing but there was a time when you could go straight down it - not that we did. But Alfredo, the guide, took us down this slope in graduated traverses until we reached the recognized runs, and I must say this is quite an effort and you need quite a degree of skill.

I think at this stage I might mention something about the standards you can take. The Swiss run three standards, bronze, silver and gold, and the Ski Club of Great Britain have similar standards. But the British ones are considerably higher graded. To take the British standard you have to be at a resort where there are one or more representatives of the Ski Club of Great Britain who have suitable qualifications to judge these tests.

The bronze standard is quite difficult until you have done quite a bit of skiing after the beginning stage. You have to be able to traverse so many thousand feet down a recognized run, as at St Moritz, in a minimum time. I don't think falls counted in those days, but of course if you did fall, it cut down the time factor and you probably wouldn't get there in the right time, so you had to be pretty good to stay upright and get to the other end. These tests were carried out at midday as a rule, when a lot of people come off the slopes and start having their lunch, but for all practical purposes, it isn't a free run - you do the same run as many hundreds of other people and you not only have to get there but you have to miss the other people, and this of course takes time as well. Apart from what I call the speed run, you have to be able to satisfy the testers that you could cope with other grades of snow, and it took me many years to get my bronze standard, for which you get a little badge which you can wear on your jacket, because there wasn't a representative of the Ski Club who had the qualifications to take the test.

The silver standard is considerably more difficult, and that again took me many years, and in fact it wasn't until I was about 60 when I eventually got it, because you have to take it in three parts. First there is what I call the 'smash and dash' where you have to do a recognized run at a resort in a minimum time and I don't think in this case falls are allowed. Certainly if you fell, you couldn't do it in the time. Then the second is that you have to satisfy the examiner in difficult snow conditions which may not only be soft snow, but crusted snow which is extremely difficult;

and there is no sort of standard for this - you just have to satisfy the examiners that you can cope, so that if you come across a difficult patch of snow you just won't be landed and have to be rescued. I remember I took my 'smash and dash' for the silver badge at Sestrière and managed to get there in time, falling over as I passed the line, but that didn't matter.

To complete the test after many years when I never went anywhere where there was anybody to take the test, I did a special course run by the Ski Club of Great Britain at Andermatt. This is a lovely village but the skiing areas in those days were pretty limited. It was a delightful spot and it was the winter headquarters of the Royal Navy Ski Club. This course was specially run for those who wanted to complete their silver standard and I must say that the chap who took us out on the test, at the end of a fortnight's training, under terrible conditions that day, took us through some most difficult country. One of the things you were not supposed to do was fall down over a course set at quite an angle on soft snow and you weren't allowed to take it straight because you had to follow the leader and more or less go where he went, and to make matters fair and above board there was a second examiner coming behind the whole lot of you to make sure you didn't fall down and not report it. In this particular test, a fall would eliminate you.

Well, I must say I found it a very difficult test that day

and although I didn't actually fall head over heels I didn't think I did particularly well; and at the end of the day, I didn't think I had passed after all. However, at dinner that night, the leader of the expedition and course got up and announced the names of those who had passed, and I was quite surprised to find that they had accepted me. So I was able to put up my silver standard badge at last.

After this course I decided that I would have another week skiing to get fit for the remainder of the year's work, and so I took the train from Andermatt down the valley eastwards towards Austria and eventually landed up at a place called Flims. This is a nice village which is really a summer resort for the Swiss and wasn't regarded as a particularly good winter sports centre by the Swiss themselves. But it was on the list of one of the Service Ski Associations and there was a hotel there which catered for the skiing. And it was while I was there for that week that I came across Dick Bowen and his wife. We recognized each other and after a few words realized that he used to play tennis with the Grasshoppers of Brighton and I used to play for Devonshire Park of Eastbourne, and we had met on occasions playing each other in matches. So I was introduced to his wife, and from then on we struck up a friendship. And as he lived not far away just north of Brighton in a village called Henfield, we used to meet during the summer.

Following that first visit to Flims I was rung up

during the course of the year by the Bowens and asked if I would like to join them with friends of theirs called the Marriotts, to go to Arosa the following winter. As I was a loner, as you know, I gratefully accepted, and so the next year we went to this delightful hotel in Lower Arosa which is a very large area and it takes about half an hour to walk uphill from the lower part of the village, where the station is situated by the lake, up this main road which ends up at Upper Arosa where there is a delightful area with a ski school for beginners. I would recommend this to anybody - lovely scenery, fairly high and the most natural bowl for practicing anything. Anyhow we landed up there this year and I was introduced to Col Marriott and his wife and we had a very good skiing holiday. In those days of course, we were still using long skis but the conditions were right. It is a lovely area for skiing. From where we were staying there was a short walk downhill to the station of the ski hoist which took you up out of the village area on to some other ski slopes, and from there you could get an anchor lift which took you up right to the top of the range of mountains, about 10,000 feet, and from there you had a marvellous ski run down with different routes back to the village, mostly ending up in the Upper Arosa in the lovely ski bowl.

We continued our friendship and went to Arosa for several years running until finally we sold the idea to the Marriotts, who loved Arosa, that Flims would be a change and actually offered better facilities and more scope, and so whatever year it was, we returned to Flims and stayed at part of the big complex at Flims-Waldhaus. At this spot there was a big complex of a huge hotel which was really a 5-star hotel, and I think the Service Ski Association was jolly lucky to be able to be offered accommodation at such a place. It was a lovely centre, lovely hotel, good food, and there was only a not very long walk downhill to the ski slopes at the bottom, from where you could get anchor hoists in those days up the mountain. Later on they put in cable cars holding about four people. From there you could get up, and finally in the later years of our lives they even had a bigger complex when you went to the top of the glacier about 10,000 feet and it was a lovely run home.

Medical Training

Medical Student Life

I went to St. Thomas' as a first year medical student in March 1924. I remember reporting to the Dean's office and being taken down to the Medical School which is at the southern end of the hospital nearer Vauxhall Bridge, and this I call Block 9 as it is quite separate from the hospital by a big courtyard. This large building with several wings holds all the lecture theatres, museums and laboratories for the teaching of students up to their third year before they start their clinical work.

I was taken and introduced to the Professor in charge of the Zoology Department - at that time Prof Rushton. He was a small man with a very good brain and extensive knowledge, and he taught us well. This continued the work I had already started at school where I had a very good grounding, and 1 found to my surprise that I had really learned more in school than the lst year medical students had learned in their first two terms at St. Thomas'. This meant that I could easily join in with what they were doing and felt that I was in advance of them.

I was also introduced to the chemistry department where we had to learn organic and inorganic chemistry under Professor Plimmer, who was a terribly boring lecturer, and while I knew my inorganic chemistry I never really understood the organic one.

And thirdly, the last subject was physics under Professor Brinkworth, who was a very live wire, younger than the other two professors, with a very extensive brain for research, and so on. Here again I found that I could cope with everything they were teaching me and taken by and large I thoroughly enjoyed that part of 1924. We were all working up to what is known as the 1st MB exam. - in other words the first stage of a degree of a Bachelor of Medicine and Bachelor of Surgery. Before the term was ended, Prof Rushton on the physics side came quietly to me and said he thought I ought to sit for the open scholarship as he felt I had a good knowledge of the physics required and stood a good chance. I was quite taken aback at this but as the family wasn't very rich, and I had paid for my first year's fees out of my small Post Office Savings Account, I felt that nothing would be lost if I sat for this scholarship. However, before that we had to sit the London University exam for this 1st MB and I wasn't surprised at this examination when I found I had passed it.

So I then reported on the appropriate day to sit this scholarship examination at St. Thomas's Hospital which was open to all students from the whole world. I don't think there were very many entries, about twenty I believe, and we had a written and practical test in the three subjects - physics, chemistry and biology. I can remember that it was with some surprise I found my old friend Bob Williams, of Merchant Taylors' School fame as a head monitor, who was also taking this examination, and so we had something to talk about in between the various papers and examinations.

I was again quite surprised when I found I had been awarded the scholarship - the Open Science Scholarship as it was called, which was to the value of £50 a year to cover the medical fees at St. Thomas' Hospital Medical School until one qualified as a medical practitioner. £50 in those days was a lot of money and it certainly helped my father and me over this period.

Then we had our summer vacation and in September of 1924 we started our next period of training in anatomy, physiology, and some pharmacology to enable us to take the 2nd MB exam in two years time in 1926, completing the first three years of pre-medical education before starting clinical work. The anatomy consisted of attending the dissecting room which is an enormous hall with a number of biers, each containing a prepared corpse. During the next two years one had to dissect and learn the whole of one complete body, and this meant it being divided into (1) head and neck, (2) the thorax and abdomen, (3) the upper limb, and (4) the lower limb.

In addition to dissection most days, and you could do it at your own discretion and in your own time, there were set lectures, not every day, to cover the whole of anatomy from the head to the toe. In addition of course you had to buy anatomy books and study them at home to get some sort of knowledge. I found this a stimulating experience, especially as I had enjoyed dissecting frogs and dogfish in the previous year and at school, and I found I had some skill, better than the average, in doing this. I was also interested in the subject as a whole and enjoyed reading and trying to remember what was a matter of facts out of the enormous volume. I must add at this stage that the whole department was run by a Professor Parsons, who was a very learned man and highly thought of in his own profession.

Now the physiology department was run in a separate part of the building. It had its own laboratories and lecture rooms, under a Professor Edward Mellanby. He was a good lecturer and quite stimulating to listen to, but for some reason I found the subject difficult to master, and I had to pay more attention and spend more time trying to remember facts about this subject than I did about anatomy. However it is a very important subject and to understand how the human body works as distinct from its simple anatomy, you have to know a lot of physiology to put two and two together.

Pharmacology was a very dull subject, very poorly lectured upon, and I must confess I only learned bare facts of the subject, and the difficult part was trying to remember the dosage of drugs. At the end of two years of these three subjects we had to sit the examination in the summer called the 2nd MB.

I must put in here that during that spring of 1926 there was the general strike which started in the coalfields and was supported by all the other unions so that the country was more or less brought to a standstill. However this standstill did not really happen because everybody volunteered all sorts of jobs and the country carried on, although it can't have been easy for the politicians to do so. I remember the first day of the strike. I set out on my flat feet and I walked to St. Thomas'. When I got there I was promptly enrolled as a special constable as I was told that all members of the Officers Training Corps were to be made special constables. I was sent to the matron's office and from there sent to a sewing department where they fitted an internal pocket to my left trouser leg where I could put my truncheon, and I was also given a brassard to wear on the left sleeve above the wrist. Otherwise we wore our normal clothes. We were promptly on duty and marched off towards Guy's Hospital where the Borough police station was situated and that was the headquarters for all the work to be done concerning combating strike action, either criminally or maintaining law and order. I was paired off with another St. Thomas' chap who was about 16 stone 4 and also a boxer as I was, and this gave me a lot of comfort as I felt he was much stronger than I was. To start off with we were sent out from the Borough police station in pairs with a regular constable to show us the ropes, but after some time, of course, the constable had to be used for other duties and we were left on our own day by day with orders what to look out for.

One of the areas to patrol was the celebrated Tooley Street, which is a riverside road running behind the warehouses on the riverbank, and considered to be a pretty rough area. We found that the dockers were quite sociable people - they didn't want any trouble, nor did we, and we passed the time of day with them, chatting, and never had any bother at all.

Another day we were drafted to the Old Kent Road en masse where there were huge crowds down towards the Elephant and Castle onwards, and these crowds were very rough and noisy and I know for a fact, as I saw it, that they had knives and other weapons and they were hamstringing horses of the police, who were endeavouring to try and keep the crowd in order with mounted policemen.

One method used to try and keep order in this Old Kent Road was by using cars, and there were two racing drivers, one being the celebrated Dr. Barnado and the other one whose name I can't remember, but with their individual racing cars they rushed up and down the gutters in parallel down the road, did a skid turn at the end and came back on the other side again in parallel. In this way anyone who got in the way was sure of a certain death and so it kept the road clear and some of the police animals were at least spared being mutilated.

Another episode I can remember was when we were all given a day off and told we were to be on duty all night, and some time after tea, we were collected at St Thomas' Hospital Medical School in a series of open cars and told to embark, four to a car plus the driver. We were taken to Hyde Park and spent the night touring round and round various roads. Hyde Park had been converted to a big milk depot amongst other things and they obviously had some advance information that Hyde Park was going to be invaded. Anyway we apparently saved the night, but it was jolly cold. We were back in time for breakfast.

I might add that once you got to St. Thomas' you didn't get home again because there was no means of transport and you were on duty at all sorts of odd hours. It so happened that one ward in Block 7 at St. Thomas', which I think was Edward Ward, was empty for various reasons, and we were all given a paliasse to fill up with straw as in the Army manner, and a blanket or two with a pillow and told that we could sleep there at night time or when off duty and that was all we were going to get. For refreshment, in fact ordinary living food, we all used the student club which in those days consisted of an old First War hut with a semi-circular top, half of which was a restaurant run by the ABC and the other half was the lounge with chairs, tables, etc, for reading, playing bridge, and even table tennis tables. This was the only place to eat really and we all did this and as I for one had no money, we ran up a steady bill which they agreed to let us pay when the strike was over at some time in the future. I forget how much my bill came to but I eventually took it home to my father and he squared it up for me.

The only other thing I can remember in some detail was towards the end of the strike when again we were told to get ready for a day in an open car and this we did. We were called for at some time in the early morning and drove down the north side of the river through Essex to the area where all the oil tanks were - I can't remember where it was now. Anyway it was while we were down there some time after lunch that the news came through that the strike was over and we could all go home. I can remember our driver, with others, shepherding us all into his car and driving like mad back to St. Thomas', people taking the wrong side of the islands in their exuberance and excitement that the strike was at last over.

Another thing that I can remember is that several of my friends who didn't come back to St. Thomas' reported their doings when we all met again, and I remember a chap called Tiny Clive who was a bus driver, while my friend Jack Andrews, who was at Cambridge at the time, was a guard on a train between Cambridge and somewhere on the east coast. There was a lot of damage done and quite a number of people did receive injuries, but none of my own friends came to any harm.

One more little item of interest: one of my friends, Pat Lowden, turned up on the first day from his home somewhere in the south of London in an old vintage car, such as you see in the Brighton Rally nowadays, made some time in the early part of the century, and I think it was what I could call a straight three-cylinder car, with beautifully made upholstery and with a sort of dicky seat, and he managed to get some petrol for this, and when we were not otherwise engaged, and felt like it, he filled it up with certainly four others - two in the front with him driving, and two in the dicky, and we tootled round places like the West End, and as there was no other traffic except buses run by volunteers, and they were few and far between, the driving was pretty easy. Really quite exciting this and I remember on one occasion three of us were sitting in front with Pat Lowden doing the driving, and I think it was Phil Hicks who was on the left hand side working the foot brake and I was working the clutch. No harm came to anybody and we had a rather amusing time.

When I was a student at St. Thomas' it so happened that I was surrounded by a number of friends all of whom I had known, mostly at Merchant Taylor's School, who because quite a number were in the special side at the school doing the sciences, were cleverer than I was and took their 1st MB from the school and then came straight to St. Thomas' ready for the clinical work. In particular I can remember the chap I have just mentioned, Tiny Clive, whose father and mother were both artistes in the theatre, and he was gifted as a musician, and at the time we all first went there we had a very fine student band in the student club, which even my friends the Andrews hired out for a 21st party for their daughter at a place in Bond Street. When they qualified and disbanded my friend Tiny Clive started another one and they were terribly successful and a marvellous band to dance to in the students' club.

There was also a very close friend of mine, P Y Hicks, Philip Yelverton Hicks (I have never known anybody with the name Yelverton before - Yelverton of course was the place we always went to for our holidays on Dartmoor) whom I knew better than some of the others because his family were very friendly with the Andrews family, and his father was a yachtsman with a yacht at Westcliff on Sea, and even I was invited down to have some sailing.

Then there was another chap called Bluntisham Hodson, and finally of course there was my closer than all of friends, Bob Williams, who eventually became an eye specialist in the Luton and Dunstable area, while he lived at Harpenden.

If we go back to the end of the 3rd year, which was June 1926, when we all sat our exams, we found much to our surprise that we had all passed. This was the year when the exams had been held on the late side for the 2nd MB because of the general strike and the general upset of the whole of the academic world. All of us who were taking this exam then went to our OTC camp after it had started, and this was the year when it was held at Felixstowe, and in a previous report I have told you what a dreadful first night we had in a gale.

Then we had our annual vacation at the end of the academic year and of course this was the last occasion of that sort you ever had, because from then on, on the clinical side for the student, you went from one course to another with no real interval in between, and you had to do all these courses before you could sit the final exam. You couldn't take time off, so there was no vacation from then on and you were lucky if you got a few days off before you qualified. Then of course once you had qualified, if you didn't take a holiday then you never had any peace until you finally retired.

I don't know where I went for a holiday that year. I haven't any recollection of it at all, but from then on as a medical student, you had to do about a year of physician's work, another year doing surgical work, and in addition to that there were special departments for the Ear, Nose and Throat; Skins; Midwiferyand Gynaecology; and Children. I am sure there were some more which I have forgotten.

At this stage I elected not to take up clinical work because my teachers thought that I had done fairly well in the pre-medical exams and as I thought at that stage that I would like to be a surgeon like my father, I would sit the exams at the time now when I was well up in those particular subjects. The Fellowship Examination of the Royal College of Surgeons of England was sat in two parts: (a) the primary fellowship, as it was called, which included the subjects of anatomy and physiology, and (b) the second and final part which gave you the Fellowship of the Royal College of Surgeons. In those days, and up until quite recently, you took this after you had finished your training, and in point of fact in those days, which were the early '30s, you didn't have to be even a house surgeon in a surgical capacity. If you felt you were competent to take the exam you could take it, and if you passed you would become a Fellow, and eligible to do surgical work.

So at this stage I elected to continue studying anatomy and physiology with a view to taking this primary examination later that year. In other words I took many months off before starting clinical work. I didn't pass the exam this time. Although I got over 60% in anatomy, I failed to satisfy the examiners in physiology. So here I decided to continue or rather to start my clinical work and to take the exam later when the time was due. I, with Bob Williams and several of my friends, was posted to the care of the Senior Consultant Physician, Sir Maurice Cassidy, and he was assisted by his houseman, Kenneth Goadby, who later himself became a Consultant Physician at St. Thomas' Hospital, and has only recently died. He lived in retirement at Rye, Sussex.

These little 'firms', as they were called, consisted of several medical students and you were all allocated patients in the ward for whom you were responsible. You had to take their medical history on arrival, examine them, and in the case of females in the presence of a chaperone from the nursing staff. Having done all that, you had to make copious notes which became a permanent record on the hospital records. Apart from the clinical examination, one had to arrange, with approval, any laboratory tests and/or X-rays, which were thought necessary, although of course requests were signed either by the consultant or by the house physician. As far as I can remember, this part of the training lasted six months to a year.

In those days, in the 1920s, there were no antibiotics, and drugs which had any effect were very limited, and mostly consisted of sleeping pills or painkillers. Diabetes was a well known disease, but any curative treatment was unknown until about 1922, when insulin was discovered and was able to be injected, but could not be taken by mouth - or rather it could be taken but it had no effect because it was destroyed by the stomach juices. There was no treatment for pernicious anaemia, which is a killing disease, until the time when we were with our Consultant Physician, Sir Maurice Cassidy.

It was during our Clerkship, as it was called, with Dr Maurice Cassidy that taking raw liver if you had pernicious anaemia renewed your life, but of course liver in any quantity – like about 1lb a day raw, was very difficult and horrible to take, and it wasn't long before the research scientists produced the essential ingredient, and it was able to be taken separately. So during that time of my life, the cure for pernicious anaemia was discovered.

It was soon after this that Dr. Maurice Cassidy was called in to help in the treatment of King George V when he had his chest complications, and he was eventually knighted and became Sir Maurice Cassidy. Sir Maurice had a lovely house in one of those squares just on the north side and behind Selfridges. I think it was called Montague Square, where he lived with his wife, and I am told he had no family. But I can well remember he entertained us students and one particular evening when Bob Williams and I and

Dr. Gbady, his houseman, were invited to dinner at this private house to meet two of his nieces.

We were asked to meet at this house in Montague Square at something like 6pm I think and then we were all introduced to each other and sat around in his living room - I suppose in those days it was called the drawing room - and we were offered a choice of drinks and a chance to get talking and to try to get to know each other.

As far as I can remember, at about 7pm or so we were all invited into the marvellous dining room of this house and sat down to a lovely dinner of many courses. The conversation continued in a reasonable way and our host and hostess did their best to make us feel at home and happy. When all this was over and we again retired to the drawing room, our hostess announced that after a short time we would be going out by cabs to a celebrated London night club. It was one of the more well-known ones and more respectable than many, and certainly not with the reputation of a certain one which my friend Jack Andrews and I went to at one stage at his expense, where things were in a basement with dim lights, exorbitant prices for everything, full of smoke, and everybody thought they were happy except us.

To resume, we spent the evening dancing with each other - that is the males with the girls and the wife - to a very good band, and I think there was also a bit of a cabaret. Sometime at about midnight it was decided for us by our host and hostess that it was time to go home, as most of us, including myself, had work to do next day. So we all said goodbye to each other at the door of the club. They went off in their cab to Montague Square and Bob Williams and I returned to I am not sure where; I think I went back to my parents home in Chevening Road.

All the time we were learning our medicine under Sir Maurice. We were taught very carefully the rudiments of medicine, and how to examine patients in the correct manner by another celebrated physician called Dr Forrest Smith, who had been in the Navy during the First World War. He was a charming man and spoke beautiful English, very clearly. It was from my point of view quite easy to follow his line of reasoning and it was easy to assimilate what he was trying to teach us.

We used to meet at 9am on several mornings a week before we went to the wards under Sir Maurice Cassidy. This session of teaching lasted for one hour and we had the ward to ourselves and Dr. Forrest-Smith, because the wards were not open even to members of the medical staff before 10am unless they were sent for in an emergency.

I can well remember him standing at the side of the bedhead, sometimes with screens drawn around and sometimes not, while we, up to half a dozen or so, gathered all round the sides and the foot of the bed to listen to his words of wisdom. The patient meanwhile was lying comfortably and seemed quite happy to be part of the teaching process. Certainly I never knew anybody who did protest and it was an understood thing that if you went into a teaching hospital for treatment, then you were liable to be a body to be taught on by whoever was the medical specialist in charge.

We started at the bottom knowing nothing about anything. We were taught how to use the stethoscope in particular, how to use our hands, how to use our eyes and how to listen. This process is simply put into four numbers. No 1 inspection of the patient, No 2 - palpation, No 3 - percussion, and No 4 - auscultation.

The inspection of course is teaching one to use one's eyes and to describe what you see and of course, later you have to write this all down. And the first appearance of a patient as he comes into a hospital bed is a basis upon which you have to judge his progress for the better or for the worse. Palpation is quite difficult to carry out and it needs a bit of practice. First of all you must have warm hands, because there is nothing worse than having one or a pair of cold hands put upon one anywhere, particularly one's tummy when you are trying to feel. So warm hands it has to be and you will run your fingers and palm gently over the part concerned, whether it be the chest or the abdomen, arm or leg, to try and get the feel and see whether there is any abnormality of note. In the case of the abdomen, this is of course very soft and mobile and you can press in and see if you can elicit discomfort or feel any abnormal lumps.

Percussion is again a thing you have to learn and your ears have to get tuned in to the note it produces. You put your left hand on the patient with fingers apart and you tap one of them of your own choice with, say, the middle finger of the opposite hand, the finger being bent so that it resembles a hammer. You tap your own finger with a hammer finger and this elicits a note and registers as either dull or otherwise, and as you get confident in this over the years, it can tell you quite a lot about the tissues underneath your hand. Certainly at times, if there is any inflammation within the abdomen, for instance, tapping it will elicit quite a painful experience for the patient, and he generally tells you so, and this is very useful in such illnesses as acute appendicitis.

Then there is finally auscultation using the stethoscope, which I don't think needs any explanation of the instrument. You put the stethoscope at a starting point on whichever part of the body you are interested in, and then you move it around in a circular way or at various angles and listen to what you can hear. In the case of the limbs and the head, I doubt if you ever hear anything, but in the case of the chest you of course immediately hear the breathing, the intake and the output, and you have to get used to what is a normal sound. When you have got used to this, if you hear anything other than the normal sound, you have to learn by experience to interpret what you hear to help you in your diagnosis. For example, bronchitis and of course pneumonia. Also in the chest of course is that marvellous organ, the heart, and as soon as you put your stethoscope anywhere near it you hear the heart beat, and again you have to learn the different sounds and the different valves of the heart, and try and register if there is any abnormality. It generally takes many years of experience to make a diagnosis on any abnormality you may hear.

In the case of the abdomen, it is fairly silent but valve movements can be heard, and if there is anything like an obstruction in the valve, these are considerably increased.

This teaching goes on regularly and you are taught how to examine the various systems. Shall we say first, the chest? In the chest you have first to learn the normal sound of the heart beat and the normal sounds of breathing. In the abdomen you have to listen for the normal valve sounds and try and pick up anything abnormal.

On your anatomy days, you learned about the muscles, particularly of the upper and lower limbs, and the nerve supply which originates in the brain and spinal cord. So here you have to learn to examine the body to see if there is any abnormality in the brain or nervous system.

And more or less finally, you are taught how to test the products of the workings of the kidney, namely the urine, and how to examine this in the laboratory for any abnormality, such as sugar. Again you are taught how to examine the contents of the bowel in the laboratory.

Now to return to the teaching of one's physician and his houseman, he too did regular ward rounds at which we had to attend, and this could be either a morning or an afternoon, and generally took about two hours, everybody standing all the time. So you had to get used to standing but not getting too tired and keeping your brain active as well. The usual procedure was that the physician would take you to a particular bed in which there was a patient whom he knew had a certain disease, such as pneumonia, and he would then ask the clerk, which might be you, in charge of the patient to read out the history you had taken about the illness. After which he might politely ask you to elaborate on certain points or he might have a sense of humour and pull your leg a bit, as you may have seen if you have ever seen that wonderful film Doctor in the House which I might add at this stage is a typical film of any teaching hospital, particularly the London ones, and applies to almost any student.

To continue, the physician would probably examine the patient for himself to see if your findings are correct, and he might even find something with his knowledge that you had not discovered, and in this way he pointed this out to us all around the bedside, and thus you managed to pick up knowledge.

This went on for the whole session, going from bed to bed, with a definite purpose in mind; first, to establish the diagnosis and the treatment of the patient, and that this was being correctly done; and secondly, to see who was responsible for these patients to make sure that everything was being done that was humanly possible to get the patient well.

During this time, as I shall recount later in these memoirs, I was courting my first wife-to-be. She lived in the Golders Green area and I had a motorbike, so that I often went to their house after a day's work, or at other times. There was one time I remember particularly because it was a Good Friday, and although no teaching would have been done on that day, it being a religious day and the hospital and the sisters being very concerned with the spiritual well-being of the patients, I happened to be there at a particular time and although I wanted to go down and see the patients for whom I was responsible to see how they were getting on, I first went to Golders Green to pay my respects to the family who were on holiday as well for the day, and I then set off to St. Thomas'.

This consisted of a nice ride over the heath past the Leg of Mutton pond to Hampstead, down Fitzroy Avenue, past Swiss Cottage, and into Regents Park. I then left the Park at Baker Street, went down Baker Street to Oxford Street and then through Hyde Park to Hyde Park Corner, through St James' Park past Buckingham Palace, past the Houses of Parliament and Parliament Square, over Westminster Bridge, and turn right by the hospital into the students club to park the bike, etc.

Well, on this particular day, I was just riding as I thought was normal round the outer circle of Regents Park, when I was suddenly pulled up by a police trap, and although I didn't think I was exceeding the speed limit, they tried to convince me that I was. The sergeant in charge, believe it or not, had the name Sergeant Christmas, and of course he had minions with him. The first question was, did I know I was exceeding the speed limit, 20 miles per hour I think it was in those days, in the Park, - Who was I, - why was I riding that way, - and where was I going? So, not to be outdone, and with the mental impression of all medical students at the time and particularly those at St. Thomas' Hospital that all serious sick London Metropolitan policemen were admitted and treated at St. Thomas' Hospital, there was a feeling that St. Thomas' Hospital medical students were fairly likely to have any charges leniently considered and dismissed, I gave him my name and home address, told him I was a medical student, that I was pursuing my ordinary way to the hospital to see how my patients were getting on under the care of Sir Maurice Cassidy. However, at this stage I did not think that it sounded in his eyes that this was important enough on a Bank Holiday merely to be examining patients, so I swung the story a bit and said that I was going to help my chief operate on these patients during the course of the day. He accepted this, warned me to go slower, and that was the end of that. I must say my fellow students in my class were very tickled about this and pulled my leg for a long time.

However, to my surprise, some weeks later I was crossing what is known as Central Hall, which was the main entrance of the big hall to the centre block of St. Thomas' Hospital where the offices and governors' hall and so-on were situated; this is the hall in which we all used to congregate to meet our respective chiefs and proceed from there to our ward rounds. So this day, I was spoken to by the Beadle, who said there was an officer from the police force who wanted to talk to me. It turned out to be this Sgt Christmas, from Baker Street Station, who was merely confirming that I was in fact a medical student at St. Thomas' Hospital, and he also said that I might be hearing more about this in due course.

So I talked this over with my friends and they advised me to sit tight and do nothing. Some many weeks later I was told that I was to present myself to see the said surgeon whom I had mentioned to the Sergeant,

Mr. Charles Max Page, who was the surgeon to whom I had put down my name to study on his firm when the time came. I found out in due course when he was likely to appear in the hospital, and presented myself to him, explaining who I was. Mr. Max Page was a very tall and athletic man, a good surgeon and a good teacher, as I knew from repute, and he had a great reputation as a sportsman and in particular a golfer. He looked me up and down and said 'So you're the chap who has been causing all this trouble'. I said that I was sorry, and he said it wouldn't have mattered so much but the police had invaded his private house and even worried his wife and he thought that this was not quite the thing to do. So I listened carefully and gave him my explanation, upon which he smiled. Meanwhile I felt a complete worm. Finally, he gave me another up and down look and said: 'Well, I have dealt with the police for you. I don't think you'll hear any more about it, but why did you use my name?' And again I explained that it sounded more important. And as I had hoped to be under his care in a few months time, I hoped this would not interfere with my chances of being taught by him. We parted on fair terms but I was very apprehensive. I will tell you more about this a little later on.

Time went by. We finished our medical schooling and we were then posted to the surgical firms and I must say I was very surprised, but very pleased, to find I had been accepted by Mr. Max Page and his junior, Mr. RHOB Robinson. So the day arrived when we met our new chief in the central hall and we followed him and his house-surgeon up the stairs, along corridors off which all the wards led. Then we gathered around the first bedside and he from his height, standing very straight, looked us all over and I imagine he thought we were a peculiar bunch, and then he suddenly spotted my face, and he turned to me and said: 'Hallo, Wilson, what are you doing here? Is this one of your safety moves?' And of course as all my fellow students knew the story, everybody burst out laughing and that was the end of that sad episode. He was very good to me ever afterwards.

I should say at this point that I felt I had not acted in a very good spirit at the time, and I should have contacted him earlier before the police went to his house, and offered my apologies. Other people had better take note.

Teaching on the surgical side was quite different from the medical in that, not only did we have ward rounds, but we had the operating theatre. Now in those days there were two main sets of operating theatres at St Thomas' Hospital, known as the North and the South theatres, because as most people don't realize, the River Thames at that part of its course runs North to South and the hospital is on the east bank of the Thames and therefore was lined up North to South. So the theatres were individually known as North and South.

Each theatre block consisted of two theatres, making twins, with a common entrance, each with its own anaesthetic room, and also of course there were the changing rooms for the sisters, the nursing staff, the students, and the medical staff, and our station in life was quite exact. The theatre work consisted of being taught, at the start, how to prepare to go into the theatre by removing all your outdoor clothes, putting on a gown, a hat and a mask, and then you had to be taught how to put on sterile gloves. Then you were ready to assist at an operation. Of course you did not do this at once, but had to be gradually instructed as to how to behave and what to do, and so on.

To start with I think the sister of the theatre gave us all a talk about general behaviour in the theatre and how important it was to refrain from touching anything, not to get in the way, and to do exactly what you were told without question. In fact you were made to feel the lowest of the low, but of course this is quite right because in the '20s there were no antibiotics and all treatment was carried out under the aseptic technique; in other words all germs were eliminated as far as possible, and everything that you used was sterilized. This followed on from the days of the carbolic spray when germs were thought to be killed off by the carbolic, but of course in many cases it did harm to the patient, the surgeon and the staff.

So to start with you gowned up in the dressing room with material that had been sterilized. Once you had put it on to cover your own skin and clothing, it was of course no longer sterile. But you were then allowed to walk into the operating theatre anaesthetic room and receive further instructions.

I had attended the theatre on the odd occasion in the days when I was still doing my anatomy and physiology, and you did so by going in through a separate door into a gallery like a lecture theatre where you could sit down and lean over the railings and see what was going on. I wasn't very happy, I thought, the few times I had been watching what was going on, and I wondered how I would fare once I had got into the theatre. Well, as is so often the way, when you are being instructed or have a job to do, you don't give a thought as to how you feel yourself, and you get used to it very easily.

For the first few days, we just stood around keeping out of the way, and watching the general layout and working methods in the theatre as a whole. The centrepiece of course was the operating table above which was a very powerful light or lights. The patient was put on this table. The surgeon and his assistants and the anaesthetist were suitably dressed up in sterile clothing and gloves, and the work proceeded. At this stage somebody like me merely hovered around the outskirts and didn't go anywhere near the operating team, unless you were asked to. So gradually you got used to the set up and you were asked to look over somebody's shoulder to see what was happening, and eventually you were asked to what is called 'scrub up' and become part of the team. Scrubbing up means putting on an apron and washing your hands under flowing, hot water for a minimum of three minutes, with soap and water. You then had to extract a cap from a sterile container and get this on, and then take a sterile gown from another container and work your way through the sleeve holes, assisted by a nurse who tied the tapes at the back, and then you were covered, having had a mask to put on, and ready to put on sterile gloves.

In those days the sterile gloves for students and even senior staff were sterilized in an autoclave and then put into sterile water in a large sink. One of the nursing staff then, with a long handled forceps, took one of these out and handed it to you and you had to get this on. The water inside the glove helped it to come on fairly easily, but you had to learn how to get rid of the water so you didn't drown yourself or somebody else. Having got the first one on, you then were given a second one to put on, and then you were ready to be part of the team at the operating table.

The team, apart from the anaesthetist at the head end, consisted of the surgeon in charge, generally standing on the right side if he was right-handed. Opposite him would be the house surgeon and one or more assistants like myself. Generally one was enough, standing where he was asked to, either at the side of the surgeon or at the side of his assistant, depending which way he wanted you to assist.

You made sure that you kept your hands above the level of the table and if they weren't actually resting on the sterile towel which covered the patient, then you held them together where you and everybody else could see them, so you didn't touch anything you shouldn't do, and they couldn't touch you. Gradually you were asked to hold an instrument, or hold a retractor, and eventually you might even be asked to be the chief assistant to relieve the houseman so that he could do something else.

The length of operations varied from a few minutes to sometimes several hours, depending on the type of operation and how difficult it was. But the session usually lasted from 8.30 to 9am until lunchtime, and then another session would start at 2 pm and went on long into the evening or night if necessary, merely breaking for tea or refreshments as the case may be. The honorary surgeon didn't attend all the time and left some of the work to his assistants or juniors, depending on the degree of their training and competence. Generally the surgeon stayed for the whole session, but if it was an afternoon session, he very often finished himself at tea time or a little later and then probably the senior resident surgeon - who at St. Thomas' was called the resident assistant surgeon - was called upon to do what is called 'complete the list'. This would go on until those who had been prepared for that day had had their operations completed. After that, emergencies were of course coming in regularly by day and night and it was the duty of the resident assistant surgeon (in short RAS) to be responsible for looking after these patients and operating on them as necessary, reporting to the honorary surgeon the next day.

So as a student who may be in the theatre for several hours, the time came when you were released to go home yourself. Of course all this time, not only was there the ward work and theatre work, but there were systematic lectures given by the professorial staff in the lecture rooms and Medical School to teach your surgical theory, and of course there were impromptu lectures by possibly a registrar or the houseman to keep you in the picture and as up to date as possible. So, on the surgical side you were certainly far busier than on the medical side, but from my point of view, it was much more interesting, and I never seemed to get tired.

Some time during one's training, one was detailed to work in the Casualty Department and this again was a fascinating part of life. You had a regular rota of doing casualty work under the care of the sister and nursing staff in Casualty and a particular Casualty Officer to whom you were attached. There was never a dull moment here, because you never knew what sort of person was coming in, with what trouble.

The sisters and nurses were very good in sorting out

whether there was a medical or surgical condition, and surgical conditions were again sorted out into an accident, or an inflammation, - such as a boil, or something more serious. When you were under a Casualty Officer, he took you with him wherever he went and talked to you while he was taking the story, making a diagnosis, arranging for any treatment, and if possible carrying it out. As the days went by, you became more responsible as part of the team, and you were allowed to be initiated into the work and became more proficient - in other words you were allowed to take a history, make the examination and report to the Casualty Officer who might or might not agree with you. But it was still part of his teaching. At first he carried out any treatment, such as lancing a boil or sewing a wound, but eventually you were allowed to do this under his supervision, and you progressed in the art of surgery.

Another thing you had to learn was giving anaesthetics, and you were given a series of lectures, as far as I remember, and given practical experience in the use of any apparatus, and were put under the care of one of the honorary anaesthetists at the hospital. To start with, of course, like everything else, you watched him do it, he talked to you and tried to teach you the best ways to use the anaesthetics of those days, and eventually he let you do it yourself under his supervision until you became fairly proficient. Finally you were allowed to anaesthetize a patient yourself   - again as I stress, under his supervision, as he was morally responsible. In the types of anaesthetic which prevailed in those days, you could finally feel qualified and confident to give an anaesthetic to most people, knowing that they would not come to any harm.

The types of material used in the '20s were ether, chloroform, ethyl-chloride, and nitrous oxide - what is commonly known as 'laughing gas'. Ether is a very volatile fluid which you dropped on to a mask and the patient inhaled and eventually went to sleep. But it was an irritating gas and very often there was much coughing and spluttering.

Chloroform was a much less irritating fluid when it became a vapour and you did not usually get the spluttering and so on, but it was a highly dangerous drug and if you put too much on too quickly the patient would almost certainly die. In fact you only used it very sparingly in drops from a little drop bottle, as it is called, on to the mask, and you had to be very careful, although funnily enough in those days, women in labour to deliver their child used to take chloroform very easily and never seemed to come to any harm.

Ethyl-chloride was a liquid in a glass sealed bottle under pressure. The top of this bottle had a spring-like apparatus and as you pressed it, the fluid sprayed out on to the mask and was quickly vapourized and equally quickly inhaled without the irritation of the ether. And so this was often used in the first instance to get the patient over the first stage into sleep, and then the same mask was used and ether was put on the mask instead. This fluid would also be used as a spray onto a part of the body, such as a boil, which would then freeze up and become frozen to the naked eye. When that happened you could then cut it open without any pain to the patient and of course this released the purulent material from the boil and as it unfroze, the condition returned to normal but with the boil or abscess having been opened up easily.

Nitrous oxide, or laughing gas, was kept under pressure in a large cylinder about 4-5ft long and had to be connected to a rubber mask by rubber tubing. The mask was put over the patient, the gas was turned on with a valve in between to make sure the pressure was not too high, and the patient breathed in and quite quickly went to sleep. This gas was used almost entirely in dental surgery for quick extractions, and I myself used it over many years, not only at St. Thomas', but in my work at Eastbourne.

At St. Thomas' someone had devised a special apparatus called Boyle's Bag. This consisted of a big rubber bag, as big as a rugby football, connected to a metal device upon which you could fix a rubber mask. The idea was that you filled the bag with nitrous oxide and you filled the container with ether. You then applied the mask to the patient's face, turned the switch on the metal device, and this allowed the patient to breathe into and out of the bag, which contained nitrous oxide, and thereby he or she went to sleep fairly quickly. When this stage was reached, the switch was turned again and ether vapour passed on to the mask and could then be breathed without any irritation, and the anaesthetic continued indefinitely. The advantage of this piece of apparatus was that all the materials were together before you started in a closed space so you could regulate the dose, and it was much more comfortable for the patient. I don't know whether this was used in any other hospital, but it was a very sound bit of apparatus.

In addition to all the things I have talked about, one had to be trained in the practice of ear, nose and throat surgery and treatment, skins, psychiatry, nervous diseases etc. We had to attend special departments for all these subjects and it was sufficient for us to have a good enough knowledge to eventually go out into the world and practice.

"Mental disorders" was the subject I could never understand and as a student in those days, I thought it was a bit of a joke. You used to have to attend lectures on a Saturday morning at the old Maudsley Hospital which was a huge institution close to the Oval cricket ground. This of course interfered with all the Saturday sport, but you had to take the course and be signed up, otherwise you couldn't take the exam. So I used to go down on my motorbike and join the others, and when it was over go on to whichever sporting event was on at that time of the year. The lectures were given by somebody who must have been a master of his subject, but he was terribly boring and I failed to understand him at all.

Midwifery and Gynaecology

I think these were the happiest days of my student life. First, because up to now I had been living at home all my student days, as distinct from many others who had to live in digs somewhere in the London area. This of course was fortunate as home was only five miles away and it was much more comfortable to be living and sleeping in the home in which you were brought up. Secondly, we were detailed in batches of students and our particular batch only consisted of two, namely my friend Bob Williams and me. This was a great boon because we got a lot more personal attention in the teaching and in the operating theatre and particularly in the midwifery wards. As I think I have mentioned before, under sport, this coincided with the winter months, as far as I was concerned, and we had to play our rugger, as helped by the president of the rugger club who was our gynaecological teacher. The nursing staff always seemed to come second to the medical students as the latter took what is known as 'first call', and the nurses only looked after their own cases when we were either already put on a case or in this case, playing rugger. So the nursing staff welcomed us with open arms as we were away much more often than the ordinary batch, and they got much more experience

The gynaecology side was like surgery. You had your lectures on the subject and you attended the theatre. The department had its own theatre in the first block of the hospital under the care of Mr. Hedley and John Wyatt, the latter being a Merchants Taylor's student and the rugger president. The theatre work was not different from what we had done before and as we were experienced in that anyway, we just learned a new part of surgical technique, and this certainly proved very valuable when I eventually came to Eastbourne.

The midwifery side was quite different. We had lectures of course on the theory and practice of delivering infants, including Caesarian section. On the practice side, when we had sufficient knowledge, we were called into the labour ward by the sister at any time of the day or night to watch the delivery by the midwives, and taught how to do it ourselves. Not exactly DIY of these days! Soon, under supervision, we were able to do this, and I must say it was a great thrill in my life when I delivered my first infant.

As we progressed, we were allowed to go out of the

hospital on duty amongst the residents of Lambeth. This again could happen at any time of the day or night, and at night time the porter came over to your digs which were opposite the hospital, and you had to dress, go back to the porters' lodge, pick up a midwifery bag, get the address of where you had to go, and if you were lucky, you were handed a broken-down bicycle with lamps which sometimes worked. This was rather fun. For the first time in your life you were independent, you were in charge, and were treated with great respect by the inhabitants of Lambeth who did all they could to help your passage to and fro and help you in any other way. I don't actually remember the details of my first case on what was called 'the district'. I know that I went on a bike which broke down and I turned up at a block of tenement flats, without a lift of course, and introduced myself to the woman at the door, known in those days as a gamp, who was an untrained midwife, but generally having had many children herself, was pretty well versed in the ways of delivering children, and was a great help. Anyway, it was all the help you got.

So first you examine the patient, make sure all was going smoothly, and this was usually the case because they had been attending the ante-natal clinic during the course of their pregnancy, or I should say, most of them did. So then you got things ready with the gamp, got lots of boiled water on tap, put on your sterile gloves and made your examination, got the patient in the right position if possible and waited, sometimes for hours. Generally these were hand picked cases for us to look after. Most of them had had an infant previously and there weren't any complications in the ante-natal clinic and generally the birth was reasonably straightforward. It was the custom in those days that whatever the health of the patient, you gave them an enema to empty the bowel and this added to the fun of life, as it often went wrong and there was a bit of a kerfuffle everywhere. However, in this particular case, all went well, the babe was delivered wrapped up weighed, notes made and so on, and finally the babe was handed to the mother, who had no further complications, and was delighted with the treatment by her so-called 'doctor'. I might add that everybody referred to you as 'doctor'. After this, there was a general clear up. It was a custom, which the gamp had already laid on, to have brandy for the mother and brandy for the gamp, and more or less anything you wanted yourself. Sometimes the husband came along if he happened to be either out of work or off work, and a joyous celebration occurred in the small flat.

I don't know how many babies I delivered in the district altogether, but it was great fun as far as I was concerned, and the only other case I can remember is when I had a woman who delivered twins, which I think wasn't known to the staff at the hospital, and as was the custom, you sent a message to the sister in charge of the department at the hospital, who eventually sent one of the more experienced nurses out to make sure that all was going well, as this was regarded as something out of the ordinary. As far as I know, the twins survived and grew up.

The digs I mentioned before were in a row of terraced houses bang opposite the main entrance to the hospital. The type of house had a semi-basement and three storeys, with a small garden, and I think there was an indoor 'loo', as I don't remember going outside for that. The digs consisted of a big sitting room overlooking the main road, and two bedrooms for the people sharing the digs - in this case Bob Williams and myself. Visitors of the female sex were frowned upon by the landlady unless you got into her good books, which we managed to do, but we were very severely supervised. The sitting room had an open fire, with two wicker armchairs, a table in case you wanted to write or eat, and lamps, a bookcase and so on. Quite elementary stuff, though quite adequate and comfortable, especially with the open fire for which the coal was provided and no doubt we paid for. A lot of social life went on amongst ourselves and various people in the various rooms, but there wasn't all that amount of time for socializing - you always seemed to be on duty to be available for one thing or another. The thing I particularly enjoyed was going up to the main ward when you weren't busy after tea in the evening, and learning to look after and bathe the young infant, under the careful guidance of the nursing staff. This was most enjoyable and you certainly learned how to look after an infant in its early stages, and there was a little social life with the young nurses, and every now and again you had a pot of tea and so on. In fact a lot of engagements for weddings were made this way, but this didn't happen to Bob and me because he was already engaged to his Edna and I was courting my own girl.

When you lived in digs you had to find your own food which we did in the students' club, although I believe we were given breakfast in the mornings but I cannot really remember. If you wanted the bath, as distinct from a wash in your bedroom with either tepid or cold water in the hand basin on a stand, you had to cross the main road into the Casualty Department of the hospital, where in the semi-basement there was a large bathroom department, two or three bathrooms, showers, lavatories, and so on, which were used by any male person like the porters, but not patients. Anyway these were jolly good baths. There was always hot water on tap and it didn't cost you anything. But to get there you had to cross Stangate, which joined up with Westminster Bridge Road, and the other end at Vauxhall Bridge and Lambeth Bridge. In those days this was a very wide road and it was used by the London tramways - a very busy tramway which went on until about 1 or 2am and started again about 5am. Fortunately our bedrooms were at the back of the house and we didn't hear much of this night-time traffic, but it was quite a sight to see chaps like ourselves wandering across at any hour of the day or night in a dressing gown with a sponge-bag and towel to go and get a bath, because when you were on 'Midder' in particular you didn't know when you were going to get your next bath. Somewhere I have a picture of one of us crossing this road suitably attired.

Primary Fellowship

During the early part of my clinical training - I think it was certainly when I was doing the medical part of my training - I re-sat the examination called the primary fellowship - anatomy and physiology - of the Royal College of Surgeons. Having done some clinical work, I had a lot more confidence and this time I managed to pass the examination and I know I got over 60 per cent in the anatomy side. So now I was on the way to taking up a surgical career, if I so desired.

The time eventually came when we had done all the main training in the special departments and had been what is called 'signed up' for them and the time had arrived to put in an application to take the final examination to enable one to become qualified as a medical practitioner. As I recollect, one had to do a minimum of five and a half years from the start of one's training before one could sit the examination. As I started in March 1924, this was getting towards the end of 1929 and I had done the necessary time and taken the necessary courses, although at one stage I had taken six months off to do a special exam. But this wasn't spotted by the Dean and his office staff. I didn't think I was all that confident, so I thought I would take the exam in parts. In other words, medicine, or surgery, and midder, which you could do. This exam was the final exam for what was known as the Royal Colleges - in other words, the Royal College of Physicians in London, and the Royal College of Surgeons of England, who are allowed by statute to set their own exams and maintain their own standards. The qualifications being MRCS, which stands for Member of the Royal College of Surgeons, and LRCP, which is Licentiate of the Royal College of Physicians. Having passed both these exams, you are entitled to practise on the public. I put in papers to the surgical and gynaecological/midwifery side only for the MRCS. But a few days later I was horrified to find that a funny little man of small stature, whom we students used to call the Foetus, had put in to take all parts of all the exams at the same time. As he had been in my class from the beginning and was quite a brainy individual, and took most of the prizes, I was so annoyed at this that I went back to the Dean's office and signed up to take the whole exam, being very piqued.

I sat this exam of the Royal Colleges, I think, in November 1929 and to my surprise I passed in all parts, and therefore was now a qualified medical practitioner and could practise the art of medicine and surgery on the general public, should they wish to come and see me. However, before this could be authorized, I had to register my name and qualifications and all particulars with the General Medical Council, which keeps a register of all qualified medical people in this country and gives them the authority to practise, and it is of course this GMC which can strike your name off the register for a misdemeanor after anybody has made a complaint about you which justifies that act.

I think my family were as excited as I was but again I don't remember doing any special celebrations because there wasn't any money to spare and my father was a hard-working general practitioner-surgeon in the Willesden area of London, and I think we just all carried on with our normal life.

I applied for various simple appointments at St. Thomas' Hospital, which they called clinical assistants to various honorary consultants in all the various sections and grades of medicine, and I was granted the position of clinical assistant to the Children's Department, which I thought would be very useful in the future.

I believe that some time after qualifying I had a break and a holiday with my friend Jack Andrews, which I think was at Bournemouth because I remember we used to go off and play golf at Ferndown which is a little way inland from Bournemouth.

It was while I was on this short break that I received a telegram from St. Thomas' Hospital to tell me that I had been appointed to this post in the Children's Department and that I should return, in their words, 'forthwith'. Neither Jack nor I really decided what 'forthwith' meant and so we finished our weekend golfing holiday and set forth back to London. I can remember that holiday well because the Andrews family had this delightful Humber 2-seater that I would call a cabriolet. It could hold three but was really only made for two and there was a dickey behind. It had a purpose-made body by one of the major body firms like Hooper and it was beautifully fitted out and very comfortable to drive in. Jack did most of the driving as it was their family car, but I was allowed to take a turn when he felt a bit tired.

When we got back to London I reported to St. Thomas' Hospital and was told I could start working in the Children's Department that day. This appointment lasted for six months, which would bring me to about the middle of 1930 and of course, all this time one was still studying and attending lectures and so on, because one wanted to complete the London University degree of the MBBS and take the final as soon as you thought you were able to do so.

While time was passing, like all my friends, I applied for a full-time appointment, the first one always being that of a casualty officer for six months, then a fortnight's holiday, followed by another six months as either a house physician or house surgeon. The appointment was for twelve months with a break in between and if you could get one at your own teaching hospital, it gave you credit in future years. So I put in to be House Surgeon and Casualty Officer, the house surgeon part of it I took as my first choice with my previous teachers, Mr. Max Page and Mr. Robinson.

I found that I was fortunate to be appointed to this post, which started I think in the July of 1930 and lasted for six months. As I reported elsewhere in the sports section, it was during the fortnight in between this appointment and the starting of the house surgeon appointment that we took our first skiing holiday.

Casualty Officer

This was the first time in my life when I had been officially allowed to wear a white coat as a qualified medical practitioner. At St. Thomas' the custom was to have a short white coat. This distinguished you from more senior ranks and also made known to everybody that you were a qualified doctor. As far as I can remember the duties of a Casualty Officer were that you were on a rota throughout the week to be present in the casualty department at stated hours when it was your responsibility to see all accidents and other medical problems, including drunks who may present themselves at the front door or be brought in by ambulance. I think, as I mentioned before, that the porters were very experienced in doing a quick sort out, followed by the sister and staff nurses, and the patients were generally well set up or lying on a couch ready for you to see when you have got the time to get there, because you were never idle and never sitting there waiting for something to happen, so everybody had to take their turn, apart from the fact that it might be a life-saving measure.

The sessions started at 9am in the morning and finished at 1pm when you had time for lunch, and then started again at 2pm going on until 5pm. After this the night staff took over, although it is not quite as simple as that, but I have forgotten the details. Not only did you have to be responsible for these sessions in the Casualty Department, but you were also fully titled in your appointment as Resident Anaesthetist, which meant that at certain times in the week, your session instead of being in the Casualty Department, would be in one or other of the operating theatres where you would be responsible, under the Consultant Anaesthetist, for anaesthetizing patients who came to the anaesthetic room, and getting them ready for the operating surgeon in the theatre. The only training you ever had was doing so many anaesthetics as a student for which you were signed up, but of course this didn't mean that you were any good at giving anaesthetics. This is the time when you had a chance to gain great experience under the

Honorary Consultant Anaesthetist to improve your skill and be a better doctor to all the patients.

In addition to the daytime duties, there were of course during the term of duty the nights to be covered from after teatime until 9 a.m. the next morning, and there again there was a rota among the eight of you as to who would be on duty for the night shift. Of course this did not absolve you from being on duty from 9am the following morning, but I cannot remember that there were any off duty times, including the weekends, although there must have been.

During these twelve months we were housed at the hospital's expense in the Students' Club which was opposite the hospital on the other side of Lambeth Palace Road, and the top floor was reserved entirely for the casualty officers, house surgeons and physicians. So we had comfortable quarters amongst ourselves, with a club beneath us at which you could partake of all the social life, and there was a restaurant where you could get extra food if you wanted it. But your food was normally provided for you in what is called College House.

College House was an age-old area on the first floor of the hospital next to the Chapel and between two of the other ward blocks. It consisted of a big dining room and an ante-room, a small kitchen and servery. Opposite on the other side of the corridor were the two residential suites of the senior surgeon and physician known as the Resident Assistant Surgeon and Resident Assistant Physician. It was an odd thing that there was no bathroom, and when you were resident in those two posts, you had to go to one of the ward bathrooms and use it when the patients were not needing it.

I can tell you an amusing story at this stage, because when I was more senior in a surgical registrar capacity, I had to do locum duties on more than one occasion for the Resident Assistant Surgeon who was on leave, and so I know the problems of the bathroom situation. In my case I had to walk down this long corridor either clothed or in my dressing gown, and it was the custom at that time to use the bathroom in the children's medical ward. One turned up, made one's presence known to the nursing staff, who were night staff if you were having an early bath of course, and you used the bathroom and the toilet. On one particular occasion I was lying in the bath enjoying a soak and thinking of nothing in particular when suddenly the door was swished open and a nurse at some stage rushed through and into the toilet, obviously quite oblivious to the fact that I was there. So the question was, what does one do? Sit tight? Get out and run away? Or brave it out? I personally was not so embarrassed as the fact I considered that the nurse would be embarrassed, and so I decided the best thing to do was to cover my face with a large flannel and sponge and hope for the best. Well of course after a few minutes, this nurse, whom I never saw or could recognize again, rushed out of the toilet, passed me, flung open the door and whooshed back into the ward. I never heard any more about it and I never heard anybody mention it ever, so I don't even know if she knew I was in the bath or whether she reported it to the sister or not. But it was quite an amusing episode - in other words what would you do?

Now this College House provided all the meals from breakfast to supper and snacks were laid out overnight on a table, under a cloth, in case you felt a bit hungry. When you were doing this first job in your life at a teaching hospital it was quite unpaid and it was considered that if you were fortunate enough to get appointed, this was all in your favour for the future, but no money changed hands, so you got your food and lodging and a pint of beer a day, but no money and certainly no laundry. This of course went on for the whole of the twelve months. I thoroughly enjoyed this appointment as Casualty Officer. It gave one great experience and taught one how to behave towards other people and other members of the staff, and how to behave towards your senior members of staff as well on the medical side. Of course there were times when you had to teach your students who were working with you all the things that you yourself hoped to know and impart knowledge to them so that they in their turn could start a new career as a casualty officer.

There were times when things were slack, particularly during the night hours, after the pubs had closed and things had settled down, and we used to sit in the big high backed wheelchairs in which we used to push the patients who were unfit to walk, and who were pushed by the porters. We used to sit here and chatter with anybody who passed and occasionally organize a race round the casualty department and all the benches just to keep the circulation going and do something different.

The nursing staff in Casualty were terrific, particularly the Sister in my time who to me was a real battle axe, but she knew her job and was a jolly good nurse and kept discipline, and even the rowdies used to treat her with respect.

When you were detailed for night duty you didn't sleep in your own bed in the Students' Club, but there was a little room - in fact there were two - at the back of Casualty just off the main corridor which had a bed and a washbasin, and a few blankets, and if you were not actually doing anything, you could go to this room, and in fact you could even go to sleep. I quite enjoyed this, because although it wasn't very comfortable, it was warm and it was quite exciting in the sense that you never knew what was going to happen. You never got a complete night's sleep, however late you went to bed, and you never undressed of course. Somebody like me who was a light sleeper would hear the porter's footsteps coming down the corridor towards your room and you woke up before they actually got to you.

House Surgeon at St Thomas' Hospital

I started this appointment at the beginning of February 1931, I think, following our fortnight's holiday as a group skiing at Wengen in Switzerland. This appointment was quite different from that of a Casualty Officer. It was a much more mature appointment and with a much greater scope for acquiring knowledge and surgical expertise, as well as the ability to look after patients and cooperate with other medical staff, including of course being commanded by your surgical chief, in this case Mr. Charles Max Page, FRCS, and his junior on the firm, Mr. RHOB Robinson, FRCS.

Another advancement in seniority of the post was that you were again resident, but from now on you actually lived in the hospital itself and not as before in the Student Club across the road. This of course was sensible because, as you will see later, you had to be available 24 hours a day unless you were officially off duty. I was indeed very fortunate to be appointed to this position under these two eminent surgeons, who were my first choice, although there were other surgeons in the hospital who were equally proficient at teaching and carrying out their surgical work. But these were the ones I liked best for their bearing and manner.

The room one was appointed to was in the previously named College House, on the floor above the dining room, but in the same block where there were at least twelve single rooms for individual house surgeons and house physicians. Each room was amply furnished, with a sitting room containing comfortable chairs and tables, bookcases, and an adjoining small bedroom with a washbasin. I forget where we had our baths but I think it was down in the basement in Casualty as before, and also as before, all our meals were taken in the dining room of College House, and very adequate food it was too.

Also at this stage in one's career, you continued to wear a short white coat. When you took up your appointment, you reported to the Senior Resident Assistant Surgeon because he was in charge of discipline and workload of all the housemen in College House and you had to fit in your timetable with everybody else's. However, the primary consideration was that you were responsible to your two surgical chiefs and to look after their patients because they did not live in the hospital but had their private residences, generally in Harley Street and that area. After being received into the ménage, you were then introduced to the sisters of the various wards in which your surgical chiefs had their beds, and of course their patients. In my case, this was the Elizabeth Ward for ladies and Edward Ward for men, while the children's cots were in the Children's Ward.

Each ward was a typical 'Nightingale' ward with I think 24 beds in each ward, twelve on either side with an open fireplace in the centre, a central large washing-up basin, a central chair for the sister and the duty nurses to sit in and write up their records, and at the end overlooking the river was an open balcony and on either side of that, on one side were the bathrooms and on the other the toilets, which included the sluices for washing up all the toilet porcelain.

The sister was a charming person, and like most of them, vested with a good manner of authority and obviously chosen for this position by the matron, who at that time was Dame Lloyd Still, a world famous matron. The sister wore a delightful blue and white spotted uniform with the usual apron in front and a charming cap peculiar to the Nightingale school. Under her, there were one or more staff nurses - in other words those who had qualified but not reached sister status - and a number of nurses in training, from the first year probationer to the second and third year student nurses, each with its distinctive uniform and belt, and of course you had to know these as soon as possible to make sure you approached the right person when you wanted any help.

The beds in the ward were old-fashioned common-or-garden iron bedsteads with the usual mattresses, pillows and sheets, and a coverlet, and each bed had a bedside table, and some were lucky to have a movable table which went over the bed. Also there were one or two bed boards which contained the temperature chart on one and the relative drug sheet on the other, while above the bed, the heading on the wall was the name of the honorary surgical staff under whom the patient was being treated. In my case this was Mr. Max Page or Mr. Robinson.

To start off with, you were unwise if you did not take the advice of the sister of the ward on each case you had to look after, because first of all you had to take over from somebody else and read all the notes and history to make sure you were fully conversant with the problems, and later on as these were discharged and new cases brought in, you of course started afresh. But for a long time it was very helpful to have the help and advice of the sister in charge because she had a wealth of experience. The history should have been written up by one of the students, and of course you had to check this and if necessary to consult with the student and find out why you differed and correct it if necessary. You then had to check all the drug sheets and temperature charts and be conversant with whether the patient was merely being treated in bed, or had to be prepared for operation.

Twice a week your chief would come and do what is called his 'round'. He generally put on a long white coat and you had to meet him as his house surgeon at the entrance hall of the hospital, together with the students under his and your care, and then follow him wherever he went. When he reached the wards, which of course were upstairs, he entered in an imposing manner and the sister and nurses paid due deference as his word was law on the ward. The chief and his entourage went from bed to bed and he checked up all that you had prepared for him, sometimes stopping to teach on the particular illness of the patient, but mostly going from bed to bed checking up that all was well, that the right treatment was being prescribed and carried out, and at the end of the round he would pay his respects to the sister and we would all depart to the next ward. If we started on the female side, then we had to walk the long corridor to get to the male side and generally finish up in the children's ward, which was on the level with the College House dining room, and if it was appropriate the chief would often be asked to enter and have some tea or light refreshment. It was during this little after-round interlude, the round having taken certainly two hours, that we all sat down and he decided which patients were ready for operation, what type of operation, and then a decision made as to which day they would be operated upon. Each surgeon generally had two operation sessions a week and mine were mostly in the afternoon, if I remember, and so the operations went on starting at 2 p.m. with a break for tea, and continuing after tea if necessary, after which time the chief would generally retire permanently for the day. If there was anything else to be done, and if the House Surgeon was experienced enough, he would be asked to do it. But if he was not, then the Resident Assistant Surgeon would be called upon to complete the list.

In addition to the ward rounds and the operating sessions, there were of course outpatients, generally only once a week for each surgeon. These sessions were held in the Outpatients Department on the ground floor in a different part of the building but on the level with the Casualty Department, and it had its own separate entrance. It was a very large department with multiple consulting-rooms, and they were in continual use at morning and afternoon sessions throughout the week, including Saturdays, in the mornings anyway. Here, patients who had been sent up with a recommendation by their general practitioners, in whatever part of the country they lived, and who had been given an appointment by the clerical staff, were seen. These patients could be either sex, or children, coming from mostly in the London area, but a considerable number from well outside London, and even as far as the West Country, depending on the reputation of the Chief throughout the country. Here, histories had to be taken, generally by the House Surgeon, and then produced in front of the Chief who would confirm or not the diagnosis you had made, and if he felt in the mood and it was a suitable case, he would then teach upon one or more of these outpatients, because the students were there as well, learning their work.

These sessions certainly lasted two hours and could

have been longer depending upon the number of patients who had been asked to attend that day. From this attendance, each patient was either further investigated, such as having X-rays, blood tests and so on, or they might have been straightforward and be put on the waiting list to come in for various degrees of priority. For instance, somebody who had, say, a rupture of the groin but was otherwise fit, and had no past history of disease, could be put on the waiting list straight away and any final tests made after he was admitted. Conversely, if there was somebody who had an abdominal disorder with pain and discomfort, but who was not desperately ill, any investigations would have to be carried out before an operative procedure was done, and it would not be necessary for him to be in the ward in most cases for these to be carried out. As an example, he could be X-rayed - chest and abdomen - and have blood tests taken for the laboratory and so on, and then when these were finished, he or she would be given a further appointment to come back to see the Chief who would then make a decision as to what to do.

Of course, there were the emergency cases, and these had either been reported on the telephone from some general practitioner saying that the patient had, say, acute appendicitis. The patient would be sent up to the hospital, seen by the Casualty Officer, reported to the Senior Resident Surgeon, and if things were going smoothly, admitted straight away to one of the beds in the ward. You would then be notified to go down and take the story officially, make your diagnosis, and report what you had discovered to the Resident Assistant Surgeon. He would then decide the next procedure which depended upon the time of day or night. If this occurred in the day time and it was one of the days when one of the Chiefs was operating, then the patient would almost certainly be added to the operating list of that day, whether morning or afternoon. But if it was after teatime, when the honorary surgeons had generally left for home, it remained for the Resident Assistant Surgeon to decide when he would do it, and he carried out the operation as soon as it was convenient to him and the theatre staff, whatever time of the day or night it was.

In those days, there were four surgical firms, each with its Chief, Junior Surgeon, House Surgeon and so on. Each firm, in addition to the ordinary work which went on day by day, was on official 'take in' duty for seven days at a time. I forget which day this started, but it was probably Monday morning. During that seven days, it was your Chief's responsibility to admit every case presented as an emergency including fractures in those days, and these had to be fitted in, so there was always the question of whether there was a spare bed, and sometimes you even had to discharge somebody a bit on the early side if they were fit to go home so as to make room for the emergency. And many a time we had extra beds up in the centre of the ward until somebody could be discharged home, and the newcomer could take up a proper bed.

There were times during the week when, in addition to one's daily routine, operations were started after supper, say at 9pm and many a time they went on until breakfast next morning. This of course depended entirely upon the number of emergencies which were admitted and how many beds there were to take them in. Sometimes the hospital was full and we had to refuse admission, and the only alternative to St. Thomas' was either another London teaching hospital or the County Hospital called the Brook Hospital in Lambeth. If you had an all night session you had to continue next day as if nothing had happened and sometimes you got a bit tired. Certainly by the end of that week you were distinctly tired.

There is a lot of talk these days about the excessive hours which housemen work and the Government is trying to get this reduced, but it is not easy. From my point of view it was part of being taught. You had to learn your profession, you had to be able to cope day and night, and it was all part of your training, and if you couldn't stand up to it for one reason or another, either mentally or physically, then you had to consider very seriously whether you had a future in that sort of life, and if you remained in the medical profession, whether you took up something like pathology in the laboratory which didn't entail getting up at night. Anyhow, I personally survived without any problem because I managed to keep fairly fit one way or another and was still playing games, and I am sure if you kept fit you could do better work and do it for a longer time after hours. If you were lucky, and you weren't in disfavour with your chief, you may have been invited to assist him at a private operation, for which a small fee was paid.

Now at this point I repeat again that all the work you did in the hospital was unpaid, although you got your board and lodging, but no laundry. So if you were invited to attend your Chief at private operations, which meant generally a fee of two guineas, you made sure that it didn't interfere with your hospital duties and that you arranged for somebody, like one of your colleagues, to cover for you, with the approval of course of the Chief who had invited you. It was an understood thing. In those days there were no private beds in the hospital itself, although there was one small room attached to each big ward which could be used, at the discretion of the sister if somebody was particularly ill and wanted quiet, or it could be used to put somebody in like a sick doctor, when they thought it was nicer for him than being in the general ward with all the hubbub. But certainly there were no private beds on a fee-paying basis in the hospital itself. So these private operations were conducted in private nursing homes around the London area, the nearest one to St Thomas' being in St Vincent Square, just next door to Westminster School. When you were invited, you had to make sure of the time and the place, and turn up in time to dress yourself for the operating theatre and be ready

135

to assist your Chief at the time he stated.

I must say that I was asked to do this on many occasions during my six months, and you saw sometimes a different type of patient, not socially because you didn't see them, even dressed, but a different type of illness or fracture or something, depending on their status in life, and this again was another form of experience in your learning process which was very valuable.

Again I will repeat that as no money was paid to you as a Casualty Officer/Houseman, you were dependent upon your own private finances and helped by your family. In my case during my twelve months, I managed to earn a total of £100, mostly by assisting my Chief at operations at two guineas a time, but in addition, by writing medical reports at the request of solicitors concerning mostly accident cases. In dealing with these latter reports, you made it quite clear that you expected your fee of two or three guineas to be paid by the solicitor before you handed over the report, because in many cases the solicitors weren't of the top grade, their clients had no money, and if you handed over the report, it was quite likely that you would not get your fee. So you got your money before you handed the report over. These were very important reports, because you may have had to stand up in court and be cross-examined by counsel on your statement, and you soon got to learn that a clever counsel could pull you to pieces if he wished.

So at the end of twelve months I was £100 to the good and this enabled me to help pay for the Swiss holiday I had had previously and eventually to pay for my final Fellowship examination and London University fee.

During the six months as a House Surgeon, I entered and sat for the final stages of the MBBS London University degree. I did not think I knew very much medicine, but to my surprise I passed in the medicine and they failed me in the surgery. This was a great shock to me, and my Chief was even more astounded because he thought I was in the running for the gold medal. I must say I didn't think I was as good as that but it was a great surprise, so I had to wait another six months to take it again, and I passed.

At this time, funny things were going on because there was a celebrated member of St. Thomas' Hospital junior staff called Mr. NR Barratt, who was a first class brain and a very capable surgeon and administrator. They failed him in the final Fellowship examination when he was expected to be in the gold medal class, but to make things more odd, he passed first time the Mastership of Cambridge University in surgery, which was an exam in which they are out to fail you unless you were really top class. So I didn't feel quite so bad after all.

At the end of six months I felt I had quite a nice knowledge of a little in medicine and more in surgery and I wondered what to do next.

The next senior appointment at St. Thomas' Hospital was the Senior Casualty Officer and House Surgeon to Block 8. This meant you were in charge of the Casualty Department on the surgical side with the Casualty Officers under you and the students, and that you were the House Surgeon of a very superior nature in the 8th block of the hospital, which contained a ward which was used entirely for cases of infection and sepsis, such as boils, carbuncles and osteomyelitis. This enabled them to be kept separate from non-infected cases in the general ward and thereby avoid the spread of infection. Another duty of this post was that you were in charge of the Fracture Clinic in the Outpatients Department, and the Casualty Department, and of course all the time you were under the supervision of one of the honorary surgical staff - in this case Mr. PH Mitchiner.

I applied for this post and I was very pleased to say I was appointed, and I didn't have very long to wait to take it up. This post was also residential and you were given a very nice suite of rooms on the top floor of College House, away from the crowd and bustle of the ordinary housemen on the floor below. It also carried not only responsibility but a salary of £150 a year. The appointment was for twelve months, so I felt that I was in clover.

This appointment as Senior Casualty Officer certainly had the days filled up because, not only did you have to supervise the work of the junior Casualty Officers and their students, but you were responsible for the preliminary treatment of all cases of broken bones in the Fracture Clinic, and you were responsible for the running of the Special Ward in Block 8 of the hospital dealing with all the septic cases. This ward had its own attached operating theatre, and you arranged what cases should be admitted to this ward, their treatment, and in most cases what operations were needed.

I must repeat here that, all that time, one was a trainee surgeon and was under the supervision and care of Mr. Philip H Mitchiner, who came along regularly to make sure you were going on the right track. But he was available at any time, day or night, on the telephone if you had any problems and wanted advice, and of course if it was necessary he would come and take personal charge and even do an operation himself.

Some of the cases which were admitted to this ward were quite horrific. Remember, in those days there were no antibiotics and nothing available at all to combat infection or inflammation. There were a large number of patients admitted with huge carbuncles, generally on the back of their necks, and most of these I think were associated with beer drinkers who put on a lot of weight and a lot of fat, particularly around that part of their anatomy. These patients were very ill and toxic and the only recognized cure in those times was to excise the whole thing which could easily be as large as a small saucer from a cup and saucer. The devastation of this operation was quite remarkable, but if you cut away all the bad tissue, and in those days we plugged it with packs consisting of a mixture of pure carbolic and camphor crystals, all the bleeding stopped and this dressing being very antiseptic for those days, was left in place for many days and knocked out any remaining germs. While it took a long time for these patients to recover, it was quite amazing at the end of many months - up to six months - how little scar there was to show on the back of the neck after such a terrible operation.

Even more serious were the unfortunate people with what is called osteomyelitis, in other words infection of a major bone, or it could be in a minor bone. By the time these people came in they were in advanced stage generally of infection and the bone concerned was rotten and weak. The commonest place for this disease was in the tibia or shinbone, and generally resulted from some often trivial minor blow. When left to itself the bone which was affected died off, but the covering of the bone, called the periosteum, produced new bone cells to surround this dead bone and thereby maintaining some rigidity of the limb. After a considerable time, and after discharge of a lot of foul matter, the dead bone separated from the remains of the healthy bone and you were able to lift this piece out, leaving a large hole of course. Surprisingly, in those who did not die in the early stages, with adequate nursing and dressings, the new bone went on forming, the limb became strong and provided you got rid of all the dead bone, the tissues healed up leaving a scar.

As a matter of interest, when I came back from the Second World War, and found that penicillin had been discovered, there were several cases in Eastbourne which I came across who had this osteomyelitis and a persistent sore on the part of the body concerned which had been present for years. I adopted the same principle as I had at St. Thomas' - removing all the dead bone, put them on penicillin, and it was absolutely wonderful to see how they recovered and healed up.

During this time as Senior Casualty Officer, I sat for the final examination for the Fellowship of the Royal College of Surgeons of England. As I was a resident in the hospital, I had some time to spare early mornings and late evenings, and I took full advantage of this in my cozy quarters to do quite a bit of reading. My pet time was early morning, and I had an arrangement with the dining room staff that when they came on duty at 5.30 – 6.00am, the first thing they did was to bring me up a large mug of hot sweet tea and a biscuit and wake me up. From then on, apart from bathing and so on, I studied steadily until I had breakfast about 8.30am. This certainly paid off and I was able to do a lot of reading which had to be done to get sufficient knowledge to satisfy the examiners on the academic side, as distinct from the practical. I didn't pass the exam the first time but I didn't do badly either, so I arranged to sit it six months later, and passed. I think it was November 1931.

I can remember one amusing morning when I was studying, because during the previous night I had had a dream. I was in the habit of carrying around in one of my pockets a rather nice old-fashioned four shilling silver piece which somebody had given me, and one day I found it had disappeared. I don't remember dropping it or losing it, but search as I would, and as much as the cleaning staff in my rooms looked, it never came to life. Well this dream was quite vivid and it pointed out to me where this four shilling piece was - in other words in the turn-ups of one of my pairs of trousers. So next morning, when the tea-maker brought my pot of tea, before I got out of bed, I asked him to look in the turn-ups of my trousers which were hanging on the door, and lo and behold, there was the four shilling piece. So make what you can of that!

In this appointment, you did not get invited to assist in private operations and I don't remember that I was ever invited, because the junior housemen got their own perks from their various chiefs. But I did have the occasion to write a few medical reports on accident cases and thereby earned a few extra guineas. In those days, all fees were in guineas, which was the equivalent of one pound and one shilling, and of course in the older days still, the guinea was a better coin than a pound, though still golden.

I might here make a point of telling you about College House and its dining room. There was a very long table taking up the whole of the main room. The senior member of the resident staff was the Resident Assistant Surgeon who sat at the top end on the river side. I don't think there was any set place for anyone else to sit, except for the Senior Casualty Officer, who sat immediately on his right hand side in the first place on the table. The other junior appointments, like the House Physicians or House Surgeons in the various special departments like the Eye Department, and Ear, Nose and Throat Department, all sat down on either side of the table.

In my time we had some very distinguished people sitting at the head of the table. First in my junior days was Mr. RH Boggan, and when I was Senior Casualty Officer it was Mr. Norman R Barratt who had the nickname of Pasty - I have forgotten why. Thirdly following him was Mr. Cedric Tuckett. The first two, as was quite usual, became honorary members of the surgical staff at St Thomas' Hospital, - but of course there wasn't always a vacancy - and the third one became a Consultant General Surgeon in the Tonbridge area.

Adjacent to the dining room was a small room as an ante-room with some comfortable chairs to sit on and read the papers and have a general conversation, and there was also a game which was a West country game loosely termed 'ninepins' but otherwise I think known as "the-devil-among-the-tailors" This consisted of a square board with nine markers on it upon which you put the nine-pins. In one corner of the main board was an upright mast from which hung a wooden ball about the size of a ping-pong ball on a string with ball-bearings at the top. The idea was that you had three throws allowed and you had to try to knock the nine-pins down completely. This was a very sociable game and was very popular amongst the people off duty even for a few minutes. Some of us got quite good at this and could knock down the nine pins in one go fairly frequently. Now it so happens that there was one particular friend of mine who got very excited about this game and if he missed it he used to shout out in very loud terms 'poxit'. The interesting sequel to this was that this little mess block was between two of the major ward blocks of the hospital and on one side, going round one day, one of the sisters came up to me and said "Why does somebody in your mess keep on calling out 'Pot Cit'? Now 'Pot Cit' is short for potassium citrate which was a mixture in a bottle used to help combat inflammation of the bladder called cystitis, and this was in common use throughout the world, and of course the sisters and staff thought they heard the word Pot Cit and were intrigued. I was able to explain to them that what they heard was not really Pot Cit but Poxit, which came from the loud voice of my particular friend called Johnson.

Another interesting sequel to this particular game of devil-among-the-tailors was that some of my territorial camps when I was a commanding officer, which were held in the Aldershot area, were splendid camps south of the Hogs Back in Surrey, with some marvellous countryside and beautiful villages, many of which had their own cricket pitches. There was one particular village, I think it was Telford, to which if we had any spare time we used to go down to the pub in the evening for a drink and sometimes stay and watch the cricket matches. It was a very pleasant summer day or evening if you had the time to spare. Anyway, in this particular pub, believe it or not, there was a table of this devil-among-the-tailors, and of course all the locals thought they were king pins at it. So we used to challenge them and to their disgust a lot of time we beat them easily. They thought we were newcomers and so to start off with we weren't very popular but they got more drinks out of it than we did, so we all ended up being very friendly.

Interim Period

When I had finished my appointment as Senior Casualty Officer I was anxious to get further surgical experience and take up a post of Surgical Registrar somewhere, but preferably in my own teaching hospital. But it so happened that at that stage, there were four Surgical Registrars then - one to each surgical firm - who were firmly established because it was a two-year appointment, and there wasn't an immediate vacancy. The one I hoped to get eventually was with my old chiefs Mr. Max Page and Mr. Robinson. So I nipped around and suddenly I got a telephone call to ask would I be interested in taking up an emergency appointment as Senior Casualty Officer at Charing Cross Hospital, which was then in the Strand. This was because the surgeon, whom I knew, had suddenly been appointed to the honorary staff of the hospital and wanted to keep the post filled until such time as another member of their own hospital was available to fill it. So I went round and saw the Chief at the Charing Cross Hospital and accepted the post. This was a most interesting post to me because the first thing I was presented with was a splendid suite of rooms all to myself, and the next thing that struck me was that it wasn't a male-only set up as at St. Thomas'. Some of the junior staff were female.

I thought this would take a bit of getting used to but of course you never think of it twice if you go and stay in a hotel. In those days there weren't very many rooms en-suite and you all had to use the bathroom and toilet down the main corridor. And that still applied here, but there was no bother and we all got on very well. This job was entirely a 9 - 5 appointment which suited me very well as I could go on with my reading. You were very busy in the daytime because the Casualty Department was situated in the semi-basement of this hospital with its own entrance for ambulances, and being in the Strand, there were always accidents being brought in. It was a very rewarding experience which lasted me for I think about six months.

I met quite a number of interesting personalities in the theatrical world who used to pop in for a little advice occasionally, especially if they had a sore throat before doing some singing, but the one I remember most was the celebrated comedian Mr. Leslie Henson. He was exactly the same off stage in the Casualty Department as he was on stage.

I can confirm that a lot of these people behaved in civil life exactly as they did on the stage. There didn't seem to be much difference. I had another occasion when this was brought to my notice because before I went off to the Second War with the British Expeditionary Force, my friend Jack Andrews phoned me up and asked me to join him in a little party in London, first to the theatre and then to the KitKat Club which was then in Leicester Square - a very celebrated club. This I did, and the point I am trying to make is that on the neighbouring table after a short time, there came in the major members of the cast and staff of the Aldwych Theatre which used to have the

Aldwych Farces. I forget which particular play was on at the time, but the actors consisted of Ralph Lynn, Tom Walls, Mary Brough and some others. The interesting thing was that they were very friendly to us and other neighbouring tables but they behaved amongst themselves the whole evening just as if they were acting on the stage in one of their farces. It was a most interesting evening from that point of view.

Surgical Registrar

This appointment cropped up unexpectedly because one of the four Surgical Registrars at St. Thomas' had been given an appointment elsewhere in the country as a consultant surgeon, so this vacancy occurred. This was not the real vacancy I was hoping for, which could have been that of Mr. Max Page and Mr. Robinson with whom I had acted as their House Surgeon previously. However, beggars cannot be choosers and so I applied for this vacant post, the consultants being Mr. Cyril AR Nitch, FRCS and Mr. Philip H Mitchiner, FRCS.

This appointment was a non-residential one but it carried an enormous salary of £250 per year, which in those days was considered good money. This also meant that I could live at my old home in Chevening Road with my parents and travel to work every day, which I did.

The appointment was basically a 9 - 5 one every day,

excluding weekends, but there were times when you were on some sort of official duty and you had to stay behind to complete what you were doing during the day time and even do some night work and weekend work.

The duties consisted of being the senior of the trainee staff on this surgical firm, responsible to one or other of the two chiefs who had outpatient sessions and operating sessions. You had to attend all these, and were largely responsible for seeing that the procedure worked smoothly; that there was no delay and no hitches of any sort.

The day started with your meeting either Mr. Nitch or Mr. Mitchiner in the Central hall at 9am and you proceeded to the wards, or at least one of the wards, to do a ward round just as if you had been a house surgeon. In this case, you were in a more responsible position, and this could well be followed by an afternoon session in the operating theatre, or a session in the outpatient department, either seeing new cases or checking up on previously operated patients who had been asked to come back to review their progress, and these were known as 'follow-up' cases. The week passed pleasantly and all the time you were learning, because your chiefs were constantly imparting knowledge or practical points of procedure.

When you were not actually in the hospital, you had time to study and the hospital library was open until quite late in the evening if you wanted. Of course there were the other libraries, such as those in the Royal College of Surgeons, the British Medical Association, and the Royal Society of Medicine, each of which you could attend if you so desired. But of course this meant travelling to the place in London where these libraries were situated. The Royal College of Surgeons was situated in Lincolns Inn Fields, the Royal College of Physicians in the Regents Park area, the Royal Society of Medicine in Wigmore Street, and the British Medical Association in Tavistock Square.

In those days London transport consisted largely of trams as well as the buses and there was a very good tramway service which you could pick up opposite St. Thomas' Hospital, and this took you down over Westminster Bridge and then eastwards down the Embankment. At Charing Cross it branched northwards into a tunnel under the Strand, Kingsway, and came out at what is known as Bloomsbury, which was quite close first to Queens Square and also to Tavistock Square. This tramway in those days was a single-decker as distinct from most of the others, because the tunnel would only take single-decker trams, and it was known in common parlance as the 'sewer rat'. However, it was most convenient, quick and cheap, and if you wanted to go to these particular libraries in Queens Square or Tavistock Square, it was a very simple journey.

I should here mention about the various Colleges and Institutions.

Royal College of Surgeons of England

This was situated on the south side of Lincolns Inn Fields and was a very imposing building which had been there for several centuries and contained the Hunterian Museum - John Hunter being the famous surgeon of the 16th century who really started off the tenets of surgery.

As well as the Museum there were all the offices of the staff, the lecture theatres, the Great Hall, the stairway, the secretary's office and of course the library. It was a great place and I used it very frequently, apart from taking the exams there.

Royal College of Physicians

I am not sure that I ever visited this College because it wasn't part of the medical curriculum I was going to take up, and I know that since those days it has moved from its original site to Outer Circle and Regents Park. As a Licentiate of the Royal College of Physicians I was permitted to use the facilities of this College as necessary, the same as I could at the Royal College of Surgeons, having become a member of that College.

Royal Society of Medicine

This was in Wigmore Street and it had a good library, a series of lecture theatres and a dining room. You had to pay a membership fee to join the Society and there was something wrong with you if you weren't elected to be a member. It so happened that the Royal Society had sections of all the recognized specialties in medicine and surgery, each with its own meeting time and lecture time, and each elected its own President, Secretary, Treasurer, and so on. These lectures were invariably arranged for the evening or certainly after 6pm so that most people could get to them after they had finished their ordinary day's work. The lectures were of very high quality and were well attended.

I joined the Society at the suggestion of my Chief, Mr. Nitch, and he expected me to compose papers on subjects in which he was interested and which could be produced and talked about at the Royal Society of Medicine. I only did this once or twice because I wasn't a very good author and I didn't seem to have the time anyway.

When I eventually left London for Eastbourne I did not continue my membership of this society because the secretary was not a chap I admired, and he told me that I owed a lot of money as I hadn't paid any money from a certain date which he said was before I left London. I disputed this and had one or more interviews with him, but he was very high handed about the whole thing and I sent in my resignation. I believe I was blackballed, so in theory I could never attend again, but of course they never had any check on who turned up for lectures and one did just the same and paid nothing for it.

British Medical Association

This was situated in Tavistock Square. These were also imposing buildings with wrought iron gates and archways and it contained a very good library, lecture rooms, a big hall for meetings and so on. It also had a good restaurant. This I also used frequently and I arranged to meet friends there, often had a meal there on my way home, and certainly I used the library a lot.

One of the duties of a surgical registrar is to assist in the teaching of the students allotted to the supervision of one's chief. So apart from being present at ward rounds and knowing what is going on, and in the theatre knowing what is happening, in between whiles, somehow you have to fit in a series of lectures quite distinct from those given by the consultant staff or other professional lecturers. Sometimes you could get a few students together in the changing rooms where you had refreshments in between surgical operations, but mostly one used to have a regular time set aside in a week where we all met in the museum.

This museum was a wonderful place situated in the 9th block of the hospital, in other words, within the Medical School building itself. But of course it was used by everybody and all the specimens were contributed through the various consultant staff and processed in the laboratory.

This museum was three storeys high with a ground floor having shelves all round the four sides apart from the doorway, and in the centre other show cases which could be used for special occasions. The two floors above were reached by a stairway and were similarly constructed with a gallery sufficient for two people to walk along, and the walls were covered in shelves, each containing specimens of anatomy, physiology, and diseases of one sort or another, in their regular sequence and in sections depicting a certain illness or disease.

We used to congregate here once or twice a week, generally in the time between 12 and 1pm because after 12 the wards were closed to visitors and the time from 1 – 2pm was generally allowed for people to have lunch.

One generally had a blackboard and chalks and a subject was chosen, such as osteomyelitis and the whole subject was discussed from A to Z, its origins, how it happened, how you had to treat it and results, and so on. Generally this was interspersed with questions or remarks from one's audience, and there was always somebody amongst the students who had a bit of higher intelligence than the average, and perhaps he had done a little homework beforehand, knowing which subject was going to be talked about, and in many cases these bright, and even not so bright, students were out to catch you out. So you had to be pretty well up in the subject yourself before you started, and to be prepared to answer quite difficult questions, and there were times of course when you didn't know the answer, and even the questioner didn't know the answer. But this of course stimulated you to do further research yourself after teaching had finished and to try to get the truth so that you yourself were better informed and better able to teach. I really enjoyed these sessions because the students were basically intelligent and some had quite a sense of humour, and if you yourself were of the nature with a lot of give and take tolerance, you got on very well and could keep your end up.

A very important part of one's duties was standing in for the one and only senior resident surgeon known as the Resident Assistant Surgeon. In the old days there was only one surgical registrar who had a two-year tenure of office and who had very little clinical or operating work to do. His life was mostly concerned with dealing with records as the term of employment implies. However, in my time this appointment had been changed for the better, in that they had one surgical registrar for each surgical firm. The appointment was for two years in the first instance. Apart from the duties which I have already described, quite a major part of the duties was being, as one's title suggested, a registrar and you were responsible for your share of all the records for the surgical team to which you belonged. At the end of the year, the four registrars had to get together and produce a report which was bound and put in the archives. This report dealt with an analysis of all the patients admitted and operated upon, was classified, and a symposium made and opinions given on the work of that year.

We had the use of a glorious room immediately on the right hand side as you entered the Central Hall off the main road. This was a huge room with a high ceiling with all the walls covered with bookcases containing previous records of the hospital, and there was a series of long tables used as desks running transversely across the room, because the only windows were on the open front side facing the main road. Under these windows generally sat two permanent secretaries who helped us in our registrar work and in the filing.

This was really a very onerous job because you had to go through each person's record in great detail and make a summary of it, and at the end of twelve months, all similar types of cases - for example acute appendicitis - had to be correlated, and a little dissertation given about the numbers and the types, and how many lived and survived and so on. If you do this for every disease you can think of, it is really quite a stupendous job. It was made a little easier by the fact that there is a classical list of diseases which is constantly upgraded and you could work on this list and make sure you didn't miss anything out.

At the end of the year this collection of reports was finalized and printed, put into book form, and added to the Library. I have one in my collection dealing with the year or so when I was dealing with this, and it is really quite interesting to look back upon.

Of the four surgical registrars in my era, there was a friend of mine called Mr. JH Conyers, FRCS, and I was fortunate in having him close to me because we both got married during our term of office, and while I had a flat in Clive Court in Maida Vale opposite the Hospital for Nervous Diseases, he had a flat in Clifton Court in St Johns Wood, and frequently, if my duties permitted, we used to walk home together over Westminster Bridge, across Parliament Square, through St James Park past Buckingham Palace, Hyde Park Corner, Marble Arch and up the Edgeware Road. Only of course if it was fine! This was a very nice walk and good exercise, especially as we were otherwise indoors all day, and it was quite refreshing. It also saved a little bit of bus money. If you wanted to save a lot of money, it was difficult because it only cost about one penny in those days from Marble Arch to St Johns Wood and that was a long mile through a built-up area with lots of shops, and that was the unpleasant part.

It had been customary in the job of surgical registrar, as I learned from my predecessor, Mr. RO Lee, FRCS, for one's chief sometimes to invite you out to assist at a private operation, in a similar way as used to happen when we were House Surgeons. It wasn't long after I started my work that Mr. Lynch did invite me to meet him on a certain day of the week at a certain private nursing home in about a week's time. I gladly accepted.

However, something must have upset him, because before the week was out he cancelled my appointment with him at this private operation and in the rest of my time as surgical registrar with him I was never asked again. He never referred to it again and I never found out why.

The salary was only £250 per year, and at that time I was living at home, so my expenses were small, and so I was really in comparative luxury. However, by this time I was keen to get married, but of course you couldn't live on £250 a year. So I searched around and talked with many friends and colleagues, and I was advised that I might possibly get an appointment with a certain Colonel Harrison who was the Chief of the Department of Venereal Diseases situated in St. Thomas' Hospital, and it had a worldwide reputation. I eventually got an appointment to see this Col Harrison and he couldn't have been nicer, and said that there was a vacancy and it would entail doing work in the evenings between 6 and 10pm but only on four days a week, and for this appointment, I would be offered the sum of £150 a year. So this gave me a total income of £400 per year and I went ahead with arrangements to be married.

This appointment didn't clash with my other duties and my chief, Mr. Lynch, if he ever heard of it, didn't seem to mind. It was also a good appointment in the fact that the other full-time members of the medical staff, knowing I had got a Fellowship of the Royal College of Surgeons of England, made use of my services in a surgical capacity, which they hadn't apparently being doing before. Mark you, there was not much to be done because it all had to be arranged as an outpatient in the clinic and was done under local anaesthesia. However, it was a great experience in what is known as genito-urinary surgery and I thoroughly enjoyed the appointment and made many friends amongst the medical and nursing staff.

I had been led to believe that when I was appointed as surgical registrar I would be allowed one half day per week in which I could make further use of my time outside the hospital   This I was very anxious to do because if you stay in your own teaching hospital, you tend to get what I call insular and you only meet the people round about you and know what they are doing.

There was lots going on in the surgical world in the London area and there were lots of teaching hospitals, as well as the Royal Colleges, and I was anxious to travel around in my spare time and watch people operate, and attend special lectures which were laid on. This was very beneficial, not only to me as a trainee, but it gave me better knowledge to impart to my students.

However when my Chief, Mr. Lynch, heard about this, from what source I don't know, he took me to task and said that as far as he was concerned it was a full-time appointment and there were no half days off duty; and if I didn't like these conditions, then he would look for another registrar. Of course I could see his point of view, and as I had no other alternative, I accepted his decision and remained with him for two years. But I still think this was a bad decision and I know my other chief, Mr. Mitchiner, and other honorary consultants on the staff, thought quite differently and considered that I had been badly done by.

This other chief, Mr. Philip H Mitchiner FRCS, was quite a different type and I don't think he and Mr. Lynch got on very well together, from what I heard on the grapevine. He was very kind to me, did all he could to help me, and supported me when there were difficult decisions between the two consultant surgeons. As I have mentioned elsewhere, he had been also my commanding officer in the St Thomas'

Hospital Medical School Medical Company of Field Ambulance of the London University Officers Training Corps, and therefore we had quite a bit in common. It was during this time that he had already been stepped up to be the sole Brigadier on the Medical Services of the Territorial Army in the whole of the United Kingdom, and I had taken his place as commanding officer of the St Thomas' detachment.

It was during the end of this two-year tenure of office that one began to think about the future - in other words, to become a consultant surgeon somewhere in the British Isles. There weren't going to be any vacancies on the staff of St. Thomas' Hospital and I doubt if I would have stood a chance if there had been because it almost invariably went to the man who had been the Resident Assistant Surgeon. And that I had not been.

At one stage I was approached by the Consultant at the Ear, Nose, and Throat Department, a Mr. Neilson FRCS, who asked me to consider whether I would transfer from general surgery to the Ear, Nose, and Throat Department. I gave this serious thought because there were several difficulties. In other words, it was no means certain that I would be appointed to the vacancy even if I decided to transfer my type of work. More important still, I didn't feel that I could spend the rest of my life dealing with ear, nose and throat only, such as taking out tonsils, doing mastoids, and so on. It was too limited a life for me, so I politely replied to Mr. Neilson that I was not really interested in taking up this line of surgery.

There were many registrars in many hospitals up and down the United Kingdom, all seeking future honorary consultant appointments in either a teaching hospital, post-graduate hospital, or just a straight forward general hospital. It was well known amongst us all when we used to meet regularly at certain surgical meetings and got to know each other, who was about to retire and where, and so of course there was keen competition, and you had to put in an early application, when it became known that there would be a vacancy.

The first occasion that happened to me was that there was to be a vacancy for an Honorary Surgeon, that is a general surgeon, at the Royal Infirmary in Bristol, so I duly sent in my application and was advised that I should visit all the consultant surgical staff at that hospital as they wished to know individually each candidate. I therefore arranged to visit Bristol on a certain day and, to my gratification, my father said he would let me use his big Rover car to go down for these interviews. When the day came I set off at about 5am or maybe a little later, and all went well till I got to Reading, when something very wrong happened to the engine. Later I discovered the problem to be a little end having broken. It was still only about 6.30 or 7 in the morning and I had to wait until a garage opened before I could get any help. When I did, they were very helpful and jumped to it, but unfortunately the repair wasn't carried out and the car fit to drive until 4pm. Meanwhile I had telephoned the Hospital Secretary and told him my predicament, and said I would come when the car was ready. Of course this meant that I didn't get to Bristol until after dark and in foul weather, and I set about visiting all the people I had made appointments to see, all of which had had to be re-arranged to fit in with more or less their private life. They were all very kind to me but most pointed out that there was a candidate who already had a post at the Bristol Royal Infirmary and he was a man whom they thought would suit them very well. So I returned to London, handed back the car to my father and, as expected, I did not get the appointment.

The next vacancy was an unexpected one. An old St. Thomas' man, Mr. Dyball, FRCS, in Exeter, died suddenly and unexpectedly. Here again I took advice from my chiefs, particularly Mr. Mitchinor, who had a friend in Exeter who had been in the First War with him in the Royal Army Medical Corps. He kindly wrote to this doctor who replied that he would be delighted to put me up while I did the customary visiting of all the honorary staff, on this occasion including the physicians, as far as I can remember. So I duly travelled to Exeter, I think again by car, whose I don't remember, and had a very pleasant time being interviewed by all the members of the hospital staff at the Royal General Exeter Hospital, in the cathedral square in Exeter itself. There wasn't anybody locally who was waiting for the appointment, but I eventually found out that I was short-listed as one of three. Of the other two, one I knew well, Mr. Baron, who had trained at the Middlesex Hospital and had been in the London University Officers Training Corps with me. The other one was an unknown factor, but on paper he certainly had far greater surgical experience than either Mr. Baron or me.

The day came for the interview in the boardroom of the General Exeter Hospital. This was quite a fearsome proceeding because the members of the Board were headed by the Mayor of Exeter in the chair, and a lot of civic dignitaries who were Governors of the Hospital, and I think only two representatives of the medical profession. It so turned out that my two opponents presented themselves in top hats and tail-coats, in other words morning dress, but I was not advised to do this. When I discovered this, I felt a little disadvantaged and so had to try and carry it off with more assurance.

One of the peculiar things about this appointment at the Exeter hospital was that the surgeons at that time in the 1930s were required to deal with all the difficult and emergency cases in the midwifery department, and I must say that I have never come across or heard of this happening in any other town or city. Now, again, neither Baron nor I had done any special work in midwifery or gynaecology apart from my general training, but the third candidate who had all the marks was able to produce evidence that he had done some. Therefore Baron and I were not surprised when he was appointed. I must say I was very sorry about this because it was a delightful area in which to live and spend your life.

In those days when one applied for an appointment as a consultant surgeon, not only did you have to interview all the present members of the hospital staff, but you had to send in a typed application with all possible testimonials from the various chiefs under whom you had worked as a trainee. I must say that I was given the most splendid testimonials by some of my chiefs and these I had printed and put together in a folder, each group of pages measuring quite a number. One also had to have a sufficient number of these printed to give to each member of the hospital staff you visited, Upon these and their private interview with you, your worthiness was considered. One might also add that it came to quite a considerable expense in the days when one was not well off.

Formation of one's own Family Life

I think it must have all started with my godfather and uncle, Henry Boxer, who at that stage was probably a Commander, Royal Navy, but perhaps I had better go into it a bit more gently.

When I was a late teenager and in my early twenties, I was too involved with sports and being a medical student to worry about girls, and this was also backed up by the fact that my particular friend, Jack Andrews, was not interested in girls either, and so whenever we used to meet up and do things together, such as tennis, golf or you-name-it, girls were not in our minds at all, and in fact we tended to keep clear of them.

The only girls I had come in contact with were those belonging to the South Hampstead Tennis Club, and apart from the fact that they played good tennis, or they didn't, most of them were not very pretty, and, except that you played either with them or against them, they didn't enter in my life at all. This was particularly brought to notice when the Andrews family were acting as hosts to a Scottish farming family from Auchterarder in Fifeshire who had two, or shall we say twin, daughters who were about the same age as Jack and myself, and Mrs. Andrews thought that we two lads would be just the job to entertain them and show them round. However, Jack made it quite clear that he wasn't interested in carting round one or more girls and showing them the sights of London, and so that came to nothing.

The only other girls in my life had been in the dancing class which my parents had insisted we three boys attended, and I continued going once a week even when I was at Merchant Taylor's School. When I thought I was too much of an adult for the young girls, I joined the Young Adult class to learn ballroom dancing in a proper manner, and this I have never regretted because it has given me so much pleasure throughout the remainder of my life.

To get back to my uncle Henry: as was the custom in those days, my mother's naval brother used to come to London periodically, either to pay a visit to the Admiralty to confirm their appointments, or, in the case of my uncle Henry, on two occasions he was posted to the Admiralty for a year or two at a time, and during one of these tours at the Admiralty, he rented a house almost next to the station at Golders Green. His neighbours were a St Thomas' doctor who was a medical practitioner at Golders Green on one side, and a family called Hopper on the other. The Hopper parents had three daughters, the first two of whom were twins named Olive and Evelyn, and another daughter named Enid. I digress here to say

Olive (*r*) with twin sister Eve

Tom and Olive's wedding, with best man Jack Andrews, and bridesmaids Eve (*l*) and younger sister Enid.

that Enid Hopper eventually went to Newnham College, Cambridge, and became the personal private secretary to Mr. Gamage of Gamages, the celebrated store in Holborn, London.

After Uncle Henry had lived at Golders Green, he returned to his command in some naval vessel and on one occasion, had to visit the Admiralty for just a couple of days, and so, as was customary, he stayed with us at 108 Chevening Road. At this particular time, he suggested that we went out to a dinner dance, and he also suggested that we ask the two Hopper twins to be our partners. My mother at that time kept a very close eye on us and wouldn't have any girls in the house at any price; we had to fit in with this because it was her favourite brother. And so this was all arranged on the telephone. I think we must have borrowed my father's car and eventually on the evening we went across and met the Hopper family, were introduced to the girls and off we set for the heart of London. It turned out that Uncle Henry had arranged for us to have the dinner dance at the Piccadilly Hotel.

Now in those days, the 1920s, this was a first class hotel with a beautiful ballroom and a splendid dance band, and we had a most glorious meal and some lovely dancing. However, it was quite obvious to me that my uncle favoured Evelyn, the younger of the two twins, and I was left to look after Olive. I suppose we must have taken them home that night somehow and eventually parked the car and went home to bed.

I don't think that it was until some days after that that contact was made again with the Hopper family and I went over on my motorbike to visit them and pay my respects, and to make sure they had had no ill effects from their evening out. As is so often the case, one visit led to another. I can remember also, not long after this, that Jack Andrews and I, I think at my persuasion, offered to take the twins out again ourselves, and we went to a splendid place in those days called the Empress Rooms in Knightsbridge, not far from Harrods I think, and this again had a delightful restaurant and a splendid dance band. I can remember also that we went in Jack Andrews' family car which was a lovely little Humber two-seater coupé. With a bit of luck, they were so well built in those days, you could squash the whole four of us inside, and it was winter time. Anyway when the evening was over from midnight onwards (I might add in those days we went in white ties, tail coats and top hats, as that was the custom) we all picked up our various cloaks and things from the cloakrooms and the commissionaire kindly said 'Be careful, sir, it is very slippery' for what we did not know was that while we were dancing there had been a very sharp frost after a wet evening. The next thing I knew was that, in spite of holding Olive's arm, I went for six on the pavement on my back, fortunately without damaging myself. So we walked our way very carefully to where the car was parked and it took me the rest of the night to get home because I first of all dropped Jack at his home in Willesden Lane, No 232, and then I took the two girls back to Golders Green. At that time they had moved from where I first met them to the back of the estate high up on the hill near the Heath and the car never made it because it couldn't get up the slippery hill. So eventually I had to lock the car up and we had to walk gingerly back to what I remember was 24 Reynolds Close, and then I had to walk back to the car. I managed to get it out of the gutter and drove it very gingerly home down the Finchley Road, with a great deal of care down the fairly steep Childs Hill, and eventually I got back to where Jack's family car was usually parked in Brondesbury Park. To do this I had to cross the Brondesbury Park Road itself, which was on a slope, and get to the other side of the main road and turn sharp right across the camber and up a little slope into the garage. It took me about two hours to do this because every time I got to the centre of the main Brondesbury Park Road, which was on a hill down to the left, the car calmly slid down the hill and I had to go all the way round a big series of left hand turns back to the same position again. When I did eventually cross it, I couldn't get to the right to turn right and get up the little camber and up into the garage. But eventually I did, and I think it was about four o'clock in the morning by the time I had walked from there the short distance to my own home in Chevening Road.

One visit led to another and we then started going, Olive and I, to the student dances in the Students' Club at St. Thomas' Hospital, and finally I proposed to her on a foggy night on the outer circle of Regents Park on our way to a dinner/dance at a little restaurant in Piccadilly called Monseigneur, where the celebrated Roy Fox had his marvellous dance band. There we were joined by my friend Hoffman, with his lady partner, and we had a splendid evening to celebrate the engagement. The ring, turquoise and diamonds, had been acquired through Olive's father, Mr. Thomas Hopper, who was on the governing body of a West End stationers called Websters, at No 11 Dover Street. This firm had been going since the time of Dickens and, while not a big building, it was in the same class as a firm like Asprey.

At this time I was a Surgical Registrar at St. Thomas' Hospital, which gave me a salary of £250 a year, and to enable us to get married, I was given another night-time appointment in the Special Diseases Department at St. Thomas' Hospital, run by Col Harrison. My sessions were for four nights a week from 6 - 10pm, and that gave me another £150. So on this we arranged to get married and the date was fixed for 3rd August 1932. We were fortunate enough to be loaned the use of the Andrews' family house but mostly of the beautiful garden maintained by a splendid gardener. It also had a grass tennis court.

The wedding took place at the Church of Christ

Church, Brondsbury, which is a big church close to where I lived and on the main Willesden Green road going through Kilburn to Willesden Green, and was in a nice residential area. The ceremony took place, conducted partly by my brother, Bill, and also by the curate of the church with whom we were quite friendly at the time. After the service we all repaired to the Andrews house further up Willesden Lane, No 232, and there we welcomed all the guests and had refreshments, the toasts, the cake and photographs, and all these mementos are around somewhere with one family.

I was fortunate also to be loaned a beautiful MG car which belonged to one of my friends called Willson Pepper who was also a registrar at St. Thomas' with me, and in this car later in the day we set off and reached Bath, where we had to climb a multi-storey house to visit Olive's grandma and some aunts, after which we repaired to the big hotel overlooking the weir and Pulteney Bridge which was later taken over by the navy in the war, and as far as I know, is still in their hands. It was a splendid hotel with a lovely restaurant, and we had a marvellous room overlooking Pulteney Bridge and the weir, but as you can imagine, sleep didn't come easily and the noise of the weir certainly was unusual and tended to keep one awake.

The next day, we again visited grandma and set off for Bude. I must say at this time we hadn't made any arrangements for accommodation and thought we would just find somewhere and go visiting Cornwall for our honeymoon, except that we had booked a definite week in a hotel in Newquay. That first day we ran into a thick mist about mid-afternoon and the going was very slow, and while we eventually found Bude in the mist, we just drove up to the first house which looked like a hotel, and although it was late at night and the restaurant was all closed up, we were lucky to get a room, and were happy to settle down and go to sleep. Next day we started wandering along through Tintagel and all through the places along the north coast of Cornwall, finally finishing up in the hotel on the cliffs at Newquay where we spent a week exploring, going out in boats, and generally enjoying the good weather. On setting out for home, we travelled along the south coast and eventually finished up for a few days and nights at Little Common between Eastbourne and Bexhill, where Olive's uncle and aunt, name of Compton, had a bungalow, and they looked after us marvellously for a few days. I must say that in 1994 that bungalow is still there and the only daughter, Madge, who is a teacher, is still living in it, and she is now aged 90.

We then returned to London but we hadn't got anywhere ready to live in, and so we spent a few days with my parents at Chevening Road while I returned to work, and after a short time, one of my father's patients called Ben Morgan, who was a celebrated tenor opera singer and a schoolmaster at Ewen's school in London, was going on holiday with his wife and said we could use their flat to keep it inhabited while they were on their fortnight's holiday, before he had to return to his schoolmastering.

We then had a bit of luck in that two of Jack's maiden aunts on his mother's side lived in a splendid block of flats called Clive Court in Maida Vale, and I was told that there was a flat becoming vacant very soon and I was lucky enough to take over the tenancy. I think it was No 316 on the third floor, overlooking the west side and away from the traffic noise, and for this I have to thank these two aunts. I think the inclusive cost of the rent, heating and water came to something like £150 a year, in addition to which there was a good restaurant on the top floor. You were compelled to take the flat for a minimum of twelve months, but you didn't have to go to the restaurant necessarily because each flat had one of those old-fashioned rope lifts to the restaurant and you could order what you wanted on the telephone and down it would come, and then you sent the empties back to be washed up. We found that we could just about manage for the whole year on what I was earning, and I was lucky of course to be near our two sets of parents and so we very often had a good weekend jointly with them. Naturally it wasn't long before Olive became pregnant and all went smoothly until I had to go to camp in the Isle of Wight for my territorial training with the London University Officers' Training Corps, and Olive went to stay with her parents in Reynolds

Close, Hampstead Heath. As luck would have it, she was delivered of our firstborn, whom we called Anthea, on July 16, 1934, the night I reached the Isle of Wight. As I think I have mentioned elsewhere, all services stopped at night-time from the island and I had to wait until the next day, a Sunday, before I could get home, and by that time, the labour was over and I was very pleased to know that the birth had gone so well. I then spent a few days registering the birth and doing this, that and the other, and then returned to the Isle of Wight. I returned after my fortnight's training to find them both in good health and enjoying life.

After some days we all returned to the flat in Clive Court, Maida Vale. This was a nice flat with a big sitting room and a dining annex which was shut off with glass doors, a corridor to the kitchen, bathroom and loo, and a splendidly big window in the bedroom facing west. This was enough room to take a family. Elsewhere I think I have mentioned that I got the opportunity to become a Consultant Surgeon in the Eastbourne area, and when this was confirmed we left Clive Court in March 1935 and moved to Eastbourne. When I had been down there for the first few days, I stayed in a small hotel and arranged for the family to move down and we went to the Metropole Hotel, just to the east side of the pier and lived there happily while I got on with the practice work and so on, and we were able to look round for a house of our own. From there we moved to a front bedroom at the

Victoria Court Hotel which is on the front just by the Carpet Gardens, and I was then able to get a maisonette in Grange Gardens in Eastbourne whose front door was actually in Furness Road.

This was a nice little maisonette, with a semi-basement opening onto the garden at the back, a dining room and kitchen downstairs and the living room and bedroom on the upper, ground level. Grange Gardens itself is a big area of grass and we had permission to mark out and keep a tennis court at the back of our own garden in the main Grange Gardens. This I was put up to by my colleague, Dr Churcher, who lived the other side of the square, and who had had a court there for some years. The maisonette was not ideal and when a property came on the market because one of our patients died, I got the opportunity of taking it over. This property was what is now the bursar's house at Eastbourne College, situated between the College playing field, with its front door in Old Wish Road, and its garden on Carlisle Road. This was a big house with a cellar and nine bedrooms, with the main rooms on the ground floor; the main bedrooms on the first floor were beautiful rooms with lots of light, while the second floor had good rooms which were suitable for our resident staff, for which I was eventually able to get a man and wife, the wife as cook-housekeeper and the man who did the gardening and looked after the odd jobs and my car. All this I got for the princely sum of £100 rent per year. For an extra £5 Eastbourne College would paint the outside of this huge house every third year. The house was called Bendemeer.

[Editor's note: The Royal Navy in the shape of HMS Marlborough, occupied the College buildings during the Second World War. After the war, the College retook possession of this house, used it for the Bursary offices and for staff accommodation, and renamed it Marlborough House.]

We had a very happy life here until the Second World War started in September 1939 when I was called up as a Territorial Medical Officer and had to leave the family behind. I heard later that they had to be forcibly evacuated after the fall of Dunkirk and the possible invasion of Britain.

It was here, in Bendemeer, that our second child, Crichton, was born on 18th November 1936.

Apart from my medical/surgical work, we had a very happy life and we were young enough to be able to do a certain amount of entertaining and we often had big parties with cards or dancing, and tennis parties on the tennis court. It was a delightful place to live because we were next to the playing field and could see all the cricket, and the rugby and hockey in the winter from our window when it was poor enough weather not to go out, and watch over the wall or even on the field itself.

The house and garden kept me pretty occupied, though the house didn't need much done to it except to furnish it, because having come out of London from a one bedroom flat, we had to furnish all these rooms to make ourselves comfortable, and this we did by keeping our eyes open and attending various sales, and picking up bits of furniture and some works of art, depending on our means, and we were very pleased with what we were able to do with a limited income. I might add that having been living in London on £400 a year, I was guaranteed from the practice I had joined £1600 odd pounds for three years as a minimum, and of course as the practice increased, that was the minimum and one was able to earn more and this was a fifth share. I was eventually able to buy myself in to the third share but very soon afterwards the war started and so I didn't get any real benefit from that.

Apart from the house and garden, we were able to enjoy all the other amenities of a splendid seaside town like Eastbourne. In the summer there was the beach and the swimming and we were able to get hold of a tent which was put up for us every day and stored under the Wish Tower every night. There were very strict rules about bathing in pre-war days. You weren't allowed to bathe from the beach and if you were caught you had to pay tuppence. Also you were not supposed to share a tent with anybody other than your family, but of course space was limited as well as finance and everybody did share, and in theory nobody knew about it. As a matter of interest, when we came back from the war, the tented system had not re-started because the beach had to be cleared of all the obstacles and things. But when it was finally decreed to be safe to use the beach, I for one went down in my bathing wrap from the house, and just bathed like that. Of course it wasn't long before one of the attendants spotted me and other people and they tried to get tuppence out of us, but we all firmly said we were not going to pay tuppence, and they could take our names and addresses and let the Corporation know. Finally the Corporation realized they were never going to be able to go back to pre-war days, and the whole scheme was dropped, and you could bathe from the beach without a hut or a tent to your heart's content.

The tennis club at Upperton was not allowed to re-start and I joined the Devonshire Park Tennis Club where there also was a squash court. Eastbourne had no less than three golf clubs, the Royal Eastbourne, the Downs, and one in Willingdon, but I never got the mental pleasure out of any of these courses which I hoped I would get, and so I usually went and played at Blatchington on the Downs behind Seaford.

I will now try to describe that splendid house of pre-war days called Bendemeer. It was a large nine-bedroom house with a front door on Old Wish Road and three or four steps leading up to the front door, so the ground floor was slightly raised, and underneath the whole floor was a cellar. On entering the front door, there was a spacious hall from which, on the left side, ran a magnificent staircase to the first floor. A door to the right of the front door opened into a big room which I used as a dining room and waiting room, and this overlooked Old Wish Road and over the wall beyond to the playing field of Eastbourne College, and was more or less immediately behind the goal post of the rugby field. The second door on the right led into a magnificent and very large lounge with a fireplace at the far end, and off this lounge to the left, facing south, were the beautiful bay windows and a door leading out to a little porch and then on to the terrace outside the house overlooking the garden. From the hall again there was a door immediately opposite the front door which led to a big room which I used as my consulting room, and this had a beautifully large window opening out on to the terrace. From the left hand side of the hall, beyond the stairway which went back over the front door, there was a corridor leading to a huge kitchen, and a scullery on the south side, and on the north side a butler's pantry with little bars to the window, and various storerooms, and also with a way out to a little passage between this house Bendemeer and the next house on the east, which was the house of the headmaster of Eastbourne College. This little passage had its own door on to the main road, Old Wish Road, and another one on to the terrace of the garden.

On going up the stairs, to the left and winding round the little platform landing over the front door and then on to the first floor, there was a lovely bedroom over the dining room and looking over the College playing fields, and then the next door on the right led to a huge bedroom over the downstairs lounge, and this too had a door leading to an outside glassed-in balcony, and the glass panels could be opened and shut like any ordinary window with hinges. To the left of the bedroom was a smaller room with a basin which could be used as a dressing room. Then going over the kitchen quarters there was another big bedroom and between the two main bedrooms on the south side there was a bathroom with shower and toilet. On the north side there were smaller bedrooms which would take a single bed.

There was another staircase leading off this floor close to the second main bedroom above the kitchen, which went up to a second floor and here there were at least two bedrooms, and storerooms which we used for our resident staff. All in all it was a large, but delightful house to live in, with lots of light, and balconies you could sit on in good weather, and in fact we used to sleep out in the summer on the closed-in balcony outside the main bedroom. It was in this main bedroom that my son, Crichton, was born on 18th November 1936. We had a delightful little midwife, stumpy and stout, who knew her job very well and I assisted at the birth. Anthea and Crichton grew up in this house until the war started in 1939, and after I had been sent abroad and made a prisoner-of-war in May 1940. After Dunkirk fell in June, the family was soon after forcibly evacuated, and as I found out later, went to live in Harpenden in Hertfordshire, where my school and medical student friend, Bob Williams, and his wife also lived.

Tom in uniform in January 1940, before going to France.

Tom and Olive before Tom went to war

War Period

When I went to Eastbourne, I transferred from the
ULOTC to become the medical officer to the 58th
Field Regiment of Artillery TA, whose headquarters
and one battery, of the four, were situated in the
Goffs, Eastbourne. I stayed with them and went to
camp with them regularly until the time of Munich in
1938, but while with them I got to know the personnel
very well. Although I was very interested in gunnery,
I was never allowed to touch or fire a gun. A camp
that I remember most was at Larkhill on Salisbury
Plain, with lovely weather, and I did not have very
much to do except bring round extra comforts, such
as sandwiches or beer, to keep the chaps happy.

The next phase was at the time of Munich 1938, when
the Assistant Director of Medical Services (in short,
ADMS) in the 44th Home Counties Division, Col
Cowell, came to Eastbourne to talk to me and said
that it had been decided by the War Office to start a
new Territorial Medical Unit in Eastbourne, to be a
general hospital of 1200 beds, and whose title was to
be 3rd (2nd Eastern) General Hospital, RAMC/TA.
He then suggested that I might like to transfer from
Medical Officer to the Gunners to become officer in

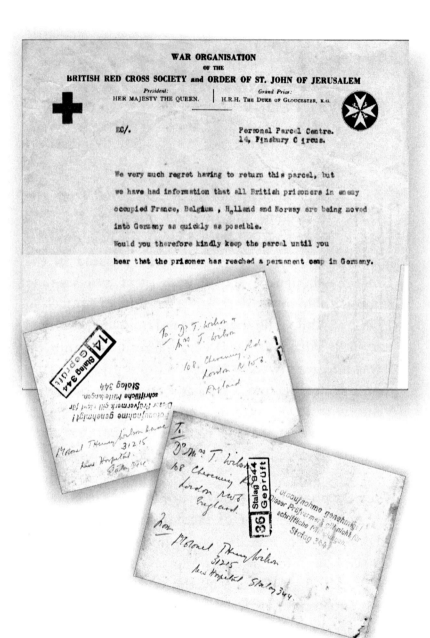

Red Cross note to Olive about returned parcel, and postcards sent by Tom from *Stalag 344* to his parents.

charge of what was called the Surgical Division of this Hospital, which carried the rank of Lt Colonel. Of course this was big step up, because although I was due for my majority, having passed the exams, a step further to a half Colonel was not often available in the Territorial Army unless you became a commander of a field ambulance. After due consideration I accepted the offer and we started to recruit people from the Eastbourne area. The commanding officer was a Col Drynen who had been commanding another territorial unit in Brighton which had been disbanded when the Eastbourne one was being formed. The CO left it to me to do most of the recruiting and make most of the arrangements for starting a new unit.

First of all we had to find some premises, and we leased one of the houses in the Upperton Road on the opposite side of the road to the General Post Office. We were sent a Warrant Officer from the regular RAMC and the rest was up to us. There was a very good fellow who had been a Quartermaster in the Brighton unit and he transferred to us as well, but that was all we had at the beginning. Advertisements were placed in the local press and I even addressed audiences at the local cinemas in the intervals after the Pathé News, and from all these areas we enlisted about 100 personnel. The Medical Officers I recruited from Eastbourne and other areas. These included a friend of mine, Leslie Lauste, a surgeon at Brighton, - and another consultant surgeon called Ralph Brook, who was in the Chichester and Brighton Area. My opposite number in charge of the medical division was a Lt Col Preston who was also a territorial officer from the Croydon area.

The local doctors were Dr Caldwell of Hampden Park, Dr Gilder of Hampden Park, Dr Harris of Eastbourne, and Dr Moran of Polegate, and the other consultant physician was Dr Alfred Emslie, also of Eastbourne, who was transferred from the 51st Highland Division (TA). There was also Dr Alderson of Eastbourne who had served in the First World War in the Royal Flying Corps and had been awarded the Military Cross.

We started training immediately and by August 1939 I was mobilized and told to take over the two buildings which had been earmarked for us at Hellingly Hospital, - one I remember by the gate being Park House. A few days before war was declared we all departed for Hellingly Hospital where everybody was billeted on the local population. I myself was billeted at the first house on the drive called Alfington House which was inhabited by the secretary to the hospital and his wife, Mr. and Mrs Rolliston. He had been a gunner officer in the First War. The other medical officers were billeted on other families up the drive including the Medical Superintendent, Dr Reid. War was declared on 3rd September and, immediately after the announcement by the Prime Minister at about 11am, there was an air raid warning and we all rapidly dispersed to our various points of shelter.

As you know, nothing much happened for many months at the beginning of the war and training continued intensively. We received our war equipment by train at Hellingly railway station and this all had to be checked and repacked and everything labeled in a code while the unit itself was designated the 21st British General Hospital. During this time we received our intake which consisted of young volunteer men mostly from the London area, and they had to be fitted into the establishment which brought us up to war strength, and of course they all had to be trained in their various duties. During this time also we were allotted a matron and her retinue of 50 Queen Alexandra Imperial Nursing Service sisters, all from the Territorial Army.

That winter was very cold with lots of snow and it was very difficult to keep warm, but we managed some Christmas celebrations, and shortly afterwards we were told to get ready to set out for an unknown destination, ready to become more active in the war overseas. I think it was 8th January 1940 when I was detailed by the CO to parade the troops early one morning in the snow and march them to Hellingly station, where we reported to the Rail Traffic Officer and entrained with all our equipment. There was only one fly in the ointment - the commanding officer failed to appear. As the Rail Traffic Officer had his orders, the train moved off without him as far as Polegate junction where we were put into a siding, and Lt Col Preston was put in charge of the personnel on the train. He had no instructions as to what to do. After a delay of maybe an hour or more, a car was seen dashing down the main road from the Hellingly direction and this contained the CO and his driver who eventually got onto the train. Shortly afterwards we set out on our journey which turned out to be to Southampton. There we detrained and we had a long wait under cover until we were embarked on a sizeable ship on which we sailed after dark for an unknown destination. It was during this time at Southampton when lunching with the Colonel that I accidentally knocked his elbow and he was considerably upset and in pain in consequence. At that time he did not say anything more. When we arrived at the port of disembarkation it turned out to be Le Havre. We were then hustled into a waiting train which was stone cold, and set off for somewhere into France. There was no news of anybody else and no news of where we were going or even where we were.

Some time during the night Col Preston came to me and said that the commanding officer was seriously ill and would I come and have a look at him, which I did. It turned out that during a party the night before he went back to his office-cum-bedroom where he slept on a camp bed which was collapsible. It had actually collapsed and he must have rolled into the grate where there was a coal fire, because his arm was burnt, was obviously giving great trouble and was infected. We managed to get hold of the guard on the train and at the next place the train stopped, we knew not where, we persuaded the guard to consult somebody and eventually we managed to get the commanding officer taken off the train and taken to a nearby hospital, but at that time we still did not know where we were. It later turned out to be Rouen.

The mistake we made there was not to send a companion with him, but there was a war on and we did not know where we were due to go and we did not feel like getting rid of personnel. Some time about dawn the train pulled up at what I can only call a wayside station, which was called Camiers, and this turned out to be about 20 kms south of Boulogne just inland from the coast, but on the main line from Boulogne to Paris. There we disembarked and were very pleased to be welcomed by our advance party under a Major Crawford who was our anaesthetist, and they had a marvellous brew up of strong, sweet tea to warm us up.

We were marched to a frozen, snow-covered field next to a series of buildings which turned out to be a boys' school which was being used by the 17th London General Hospital, already in post and working actively. There was also another tented unit in position in another field, which was the 20th General Hospital from the Cambridge area, and they in particular were very courteous and kind to us and helped us all they could to get established, and meanwhile fed us. So it was all hands to work. We had to put up our own tents for sleeping and messing and get established before we could think of putting up the numerous tents to take and house 1200 patients. This was eventually done by the end of April. There were a few Nissen huts which were extremely cold and some of us were fortunate enough to be in them and not in tents, but although we had a stove and kept the fire going all night, the water froze in the basins and one had to dress to go to bed to keep warm. During this time I developed German Measles and wasn't very well. It so happened that many of the unit had developed German Measles at Hellingly before we set out and we had to leave them behind and have substitutes, so we lost quite a number of our Eastbourne territorial volunteers.

As you will remember, Hitler invaded the Low Countries on 10 May 1940 and about this time I was ordered by the CO to go down to Amiens to welcome the matron and the nurses and bring them up to Camiers. When I reached Amiens by train and reported to the Transport Officer, it was obvious to everybody in Amiens that the Germans had lodged south of the town and were doing an encircling movement to start coming up the coast, and it seemed foolish to me to get these ladies to come up to our area with a chance of being captured. So I managed to see somebody in authority in the Amiens station area and persuaded them that it would be much better if they were sent straight back to Britain, which is actually what happened, and they were saved a miserable war and prison life.

So I returned back to Camiers, reported to the CO who wasn't very pleased but saw the sense of it.

It wasn't long after this, as nobody received any casualties, that the powers-that-be decided that we should all be evacuated from our area of three hospitals, leaving the 17th as nucleus of all ranks to look after the sick and wounded they already had. Our unit, the 21st, managed to find a train in a siding and persuaded the engine driver to take us into Boulogne, where we reassembled on the quayside waiting for the next ship to take us home to Britain. Our CO meanwhile, with the registrar, had stayed behind to burn what he called important documents. It was while sitting on my pack on the quayside that the Director-General of Medical Services in France, General Scott, came up to me - he happened to know me as he had two boys at Eastbourne College and we had met on some territorial exercises - and asked what I was doing there. I told him that we had been ordered to evacuate and were waiting for the next boat. 'Well' he said, 'I'm afraid I have got some bad news for you, because the hospital which was to cope with the forthcoming battle in this area has already evacuated and there is no medical cover for the area'. So he took me and my chief clerk in his car to the site of the previous general hospital and told us to prepare for casualties. When I asked him how long we should stay he said 'Until further orders'. Sooner, rather than later, the Germans came up the coast from the south and there was a big battle in the Boulogne area and round the docks from which we received many casualties, including many civilians and French and Belgian soldiers who were in the area. So we had a lot to do, with the three surgeons and duty officers acting as anaesthetists. As time went on we ran out of heating equipment and we had to sterilize everything in strong Lysol. We also ran out of lighting as the electricity seemed to be cut off and we had to transfer all the work we did to the cellars as there was bombardment going on at the time. Then one day all the noise ceased and we knew the battle had finished. It wasn't until a day or two later that a German medical officer appeared to find out who we were and we persuaded him to give us some rations as we were running short.

Editor's Note: My father did not include his experiences as a prisoner of war in his autobiography but he was subsequently interviewed about these years. The transcript of this interview is lodged with the Imperial War Museum. A copy is inserted here in order to complete this account of his life.

Army pay slip for Tom during his time as a POW

Prisoner of War

TO BE DETACHED BY THE PAYEE.

Will you kindly enclose this detail of the pay and/or allowances represented by this draft in any future communication with your client.

Rank *Lt. Col.* Name *T. H. Wilson*

Period *1-31 July* Unit *RAMC.*

	£	s.	d.
★ (If no amount shown, this is being issued by Army Agents)			
★Pay			
★Staff Pay or Corps, Engineer or Signal Pay and/or Technical Pay			
Command or Additional Pay as			
Allowances :—Lodging	6	19	6
Fuel and Light	2	16	10
Furniture	3	2	.
Family Lodging			
Field (for period)			
Rations			
Travelling			
Other Emoluments for			
Total	12	18	4
Deductions :—Income Duty			
(Other Deductions)			
Total Deductions			
NET TOTAL	12	18	4

Any correspondence regarding this remittance should quote the reference *BEF / NE /*

and should be addressed to :—

THE OFFICER i/c, ARMY PAY OFFICE,
STOCKPORT ROAD,
MANCHESTER 13.

Contents of

SENDER Wilson.

8. Jameson Road,

Harpenden,

Herts.

Lille.

1. Pr. Grey Flannel Trousers. | RAZOR BLADES
1. Khaki cardigan X | 1p
1. Khaki pullover. X | and wools.
1. Khaki Shirt. X | 2 Face Flannels
1. Khaki Balaclava. X | 1 Towel
3. Prs. Khaki Socks. X | 2 Dentifrice.
1. Pr Khaki Gloves. X | 2 Shaving sticks
1. Pr Khaki mitt-muffs X | 3 Tablets Soap.
1. Pr cuffs X | 2 Slabs chocolate
1. Khaki Scarf. X | 1 Tooth Brush.
6. Khaki Handkerchiefs X | 1.
1. Khaki Tie. X | 1 Pr Shoes. X
1. Hussif. X

from MRS. T. Henry WILSON
8 JAMESON RD. HARPENDEN

List of contents of parcel that Olive tried to send to
Tom when he was a PoW in Lille, France.

Photos taken in POW camp *Stalag VIIIB/344*

Johnnie Bagot	?	H.C.M Jarvis George Moreton Author of Doctor in Chains	Jock Martin	Bluey O'Mara Bluey
Major W.Henderson Major Hendry	Major Sykes Major Sleek	Col T.Henry Wilson Col Tugger	Major L.Lauste Major Perdu	Capt John Borrie Author of Despite Captivity

Photo taken at Lamsdorf POW camp Stalag VIIIB/344. The dual names for some were names used in HCM Jarvis' book **"Doctor in Chains"** (written under his pen name *George Moreton*). Tom Wilson was known as *Col Tugger* in the book, Major Lauste became *Major Perdu* (a play on French translation).

Photo taken at Hildburghausen Camp 9C on February 15, 1941 by the delegate of the Twelth Red Cross Committee.

INTERVIEW WITH
THE IMPERIAL WAR MUSEUM
1939 - 1945 WAR YEARS

I: *Mr. Wilson, we're on. Could you tell me something about your family background, please? Where you were born and what your father did for a living and so on?*

R: Well, I was born in the village of Antony in Cornwall because my father at the time had come back from the Boer War where he was a surgeon and was posted to Fort Tregantle, and he married my mother after he came back, and that's where they both were in November 1904.

I: *And your education?*

R: I didn't stay there for more than six months, I'm told, when my father moved to London, came out of the forces, obviously, and set up his plates in a district called Brondesbury Park, Willesden, London, and from there I was sent to what I call a Marm's school locally which took both sexes up to a reasonable age and, I thought, gave a jolly good education, when one looks back on it. At the age of 11, I was entered for Merchant Taylors' School in the City of London, - Charterhouse Square, where I stayed until I was just 19. Didn't do very well in school, the masters were mostly away at the war at the start of my school career and I don't think they taught very well. Anyway, I was much more interested in sport and from there I went to St. Thomas' Hospital as a medical student in March 1924, and qualified in 1929. Following that, I did residential jobs and finishing up as a surgical registrar. In 1935, I came to Eastbourne.

200

I: Can you tell me about your reaction to the Declaration that we were at war with Germany in 1939? How did you react to that?

R: Well, I was prepared for it because as soon as I qualified in 1929, I joined the Territorial Army of the Royal Army Medical Corps and we started off by running the Medical School Company of the Field Ambulance in the Territorial Army. Then when I came to Eastbourne in '35, I transferred to the local field regiment of the Royal Artillery. But after Munich, I was more or less hauled out on the advice of my ADMS because they were forming a new unit in Eastbourne, a medical unit, which was called The Third (Second Eastern) General Hospital. I agreed to be posted to that with an increase in rank, or rise in rank, to Lieutenant Colonel in charge of the Surgical Division of this Hospital. After that, I had to go around Eastbourne and find places where we could be mobilized if necessary and that's it. It had all been arranged that we would mobilize at Hellingly Mental Hospital. So when war was declared, I was actually in Hellingly Mental Hospital, arranging for troops, which had been mobilized at least a week before war was declared, to receive the body of the troops ready for war.

I: What was the general atmosphere amongst the troops towards the war? Was it one of resignation or enthusiasm or what?

R: Well I think everybody was a bit prepared for it and the troops we had at that time, of course, were Territorial volunteers and they knew, - well, they thought they knew - what was going to happen and they wanted to help the country. So I think they were just resigned to it and prepared to do their bit.

I: *What were more specifically your duties at that time?*

R: We hadn't got any equipment then and the duties were to get the chaps trained in medical work in one form or another, ready to receive casualties somewhere. Doctors themselves, of course, were already trained. You don't have to train another doctor any more but some of them hadn't any idea how to salute for instance, but that was just by the way. Then they had to get used to doing military work, obeying somebody's command and fitting in, but basically the training was done by the doctors of the rank and file in nursing. Not only that, of course, but you had to have a clerical staff. You had to have cooks. All these had to be got ready to be an independent unit wherever you're put. And from then on we started receiving equipment which we had to open up, check everything, and eventually repack it to go abroad.

I: *Were you satisfied with the equipment at your disposal?*

R: Oh, very good! Very good equipment, which could be used in any part of the world, from a pair of scissors to an x-ray machine.

I: *And when did you actually go to France?*

R: Our complement was completed by what I call an intake of young chaps who enlisted and were posted with our medical core. Most of them hadn't been anywhere to be trained and we had to do the training. We had them in a reasonable state of preparedness and we went to France, I think it was the 7th of January, from Hellingly Railway Station.

I: *From where?*

R: Hellingly. It's 10 miles in the country, north of Eastbourne; it's still there.

I: *Did the move go smoothly?*

R: Yes, very smooth. All apart from the fact the CO didn't turn up, and as I was the next senior in rank, I had to march them to the station and entrain them and, of course, the train turned up with a Transport Officer, and at the appointed time off we went without any CO.

I: *What had happened to him?*

R: Well, it so happened that the last night in, everybody had to stay in the mess that night or in their digs or somewhere, ready for next morning and there was a bit of a party, of course, - there always is. I don't think the CO did anything other than any other than CO or any other member of the mess would have done but he didn't turn up in the morning and when they went to find him, they found him very ill. What had happened was that we all had camp beds and he was a big chap, about 6 foot 2 and about

about 15 stone, and his camp bed had collapsed and he'd rolled towards the fireplace and burnt his arm. Anyway, they got going well enough to meet the train at Polegate Junction, where we had to wait but it was quite obvious that he was an ill man when he came on the train. He came across on the boat with us and on the train through France. But we had to put him up in the middle of the night. We didn't know where we were; we found out afterwards that it was at Rouen, and he eventually died in a French hospital. So again, I was left in command until they appointed somebody to take his place. Apart from that, the move went very smoothly!

I: *Were you long before you went up onto the so-called Gott Line?*

R: No, we were never up there. When we landed up in the early hours of the morning, we found ourselves a place called Camiers, which is on the main line from Boulogne for Paris, but just behind the coast, and we were told to set up our hospital there and were given a pitch in a field. From then on we set about putting up all the tents, not only for the chaps to live in but for the patients to be in - these big hospital extending marquees. In the meanwhile we were camped down in rather cold Nissen huts, and the weather was terribly cold with lots of snow. We had a guard on all night, going around keeping the fires going, but even in the huts the water froze in spite of the fire. This was 1940. However, over the weeks and months, the hospital was put up as a tented hospital, and we were prepared to receive casualties.

I: *Who were the personnel in charge?*

R: Eventually they produced another Territorial officer to be in command of the unit. He was a very nice chap, a Colonel Robertson who had been ADMS of the 51st Highland Division and I think they thought he was a bit elderly for front line work and so he was posted to us. He hated this, naturally, because he wanted to be with his own Scotsmen in the front line, and I don't think he took very kindly to us, - not that he wasn't a nice enough chap to get on with. He was eventually taken prisoner and died in prison life. Another thing is that when we landed in this place Camiers, and daylight came out, we realized that we weren't alone - there were two other units there, two other general hospitals, one in tents like ourselves, - No 20 from Cambridge, a lot of whose medical officers I knew personally; and in buildings which had been a children's school, a residential school, the 17th London was working there and actually had casualties. Our particular unit, the Third (Second Eastern) General Hospital, was renamed '21' but we never ever had a casualty in the time we were there. Then, of course, Hitler invaded the Low Countries on the 10th of May and we were ready for anything that might happen. We were bombed; they didn't actually hit anything. They hit the railway on the level crossing next door to us.

I: *Were you showing red crosses?*

R: Yes. It's not evident that they went for the hospitals. They were going for the railway as they hit the railway anyway. After several days, it was obvious that the German offensive was going very well and an interesting thing happened. I was sent by my CO to go down to Amien and pick up matron and 50 female nurses of the QA Territorials. But I got there, - I forget the date now - and met the matron and her 50 charges, but in the meanwhile I'd found out from various people like Transport Officers that the Germans weren't far south of us. And so I got hold of somebody in authority and said I wouldn't receive these sisters, because where I was taking them to, we were going to be cut off and they'd be captured. So he got them on the next train back and they got back to Britain. And then a day came when we were told to evacuate; the whole lot of us, all three hospitals, with the exception that number 17 had to leave a nucleus of staff and surgeons to cope with the casualties they'd already got and for incoming ones that might occur. The 20th General Hospital managed to get back to Cambridge without trouble. Our particular year, the 21st, we managed to cadge a lift on a train which was on a siding and got into Boulogne. Without any equipment, - just what you could carry. We were all on the quay side waiting for the next boat that might come in to evacuate us, and suddenly, the senior General of the Medical Services turned up and saw me sitting on my pack, and he happened to know me because he had two boys at Eastbourne College and he'd met me as a Territorial. This was General Scott, who was the Director General of Medical Services with the BEF and he told me the sad story that the hospital which had been there to cover the area had evacuated - I rather gather, without orders from him. So he put me in his staff car and said, 'I'll show you where to go and I'll leave one of my chaps to march the troops to where you're going to be'. On the way up to this place, which happened to be a boys' school on one of the steep hills near the citadel, we ourselves got bombed and nearly got hit but managed to get there, and the troops followed on foot. This school had been left just as they'd evacuated it in a hurry; the breakfast things were still on the table and the beds of chaps that had already got out of bed and thrown things back, and there was nobody there at all. So we took over. He said, 'Goodbye' and I said, 'How long do we stay here'? And he said, 'Until further orders'. And very soon afterwards, we started receiving casualties. And this went on until the battle was finished, about the 24th of May, I think it was. We took in all sorts of casualties: British, French, Belgians, civilians, children. The facilities were pretty limited. The previous unit had put up a room as an operating theatre, really camp equipment for tented hospitals. From that point of view, it worked well, but we were short of water; we were short of fuel; we were short of lights; and we operated more or less day and night and finally, even by candles or anything we could get hold of, in the basement, because we were in a line of fire from various things. We went on until the battle was obviously over. Everything went quiet. During that time we gradually evacuated the hospital as far as we could. We sent on stretcher parties down, four men to a stretcher, with a wounded chap on it. Any walking wounded, who could hold a handle of a stretcher, was conscripted to take one down to the docks, and gradually we got rid of a lot of patients and most of the medical and nursing staff, leaving behind the chaps we thought were the key people. The COs stayed, of course, with myself as the senior surgeon, two other surgeons, - one from Brighton and one from Eastbourne, two chaps acting as a anaesthetists, medical officers, and the padre who did his work and actually gave some anaesthetics as well when we were hard pressed. And that's how we were left. At the end of the battle, we had just a few surgical staff, some orderlies who looked after the dressings and this, that and the other, the padre and no food, no water and no lights. Eventually a party of Germans arrived with an officer in charge, who asked me who the blazes we were and why we still had our Union Jack flying, and so we told him. He didn't believe us. All he was really interested in was where was our radio set for communications. And this was interesting because no British unit like that had a radio set, certainly not a transmitting one, whereas the Germans all had. And we eventually made him see daylight but we had a lot of serious casualties. We wanted rations; we wanted water; we wanted help. And they did rally around and got us enough to keep us going.

I: *What was his demeanour when he first came in?*

R: Oh, a bit truculent. You know, we were prisoners (he chuckles) and then he saw that we weren't fighting troops and all the chaps were really wounded and not scrimshanking, and he must have made some sort of reasonable report. That went on for some days and eventually the Germans reappeared and said, 'Collect all your walking wounded, we're going to march them out', which they did in spite of our remonstrances that a lot of them weren't really fit. And then we were left with a lot of bedridden people, including civilians. Eventually they moved us all by ambulance, our own captured ambulances, and we were taken back to where we'd come from at Camiers. This was the centre of the area which was already working with the 17th London and my friend Colonel Bill Tucker who was one time captain of Cambridge at rugger and played for England. We didn't use our tented hospitals; we kept on using the school buildings and we had a lot of casualties there, so there were really two units, or the remains of two units, combined there with a lot of other doctors who were brought in from other places after being captured, and we had a lot of serious cases, - broken limbs and abdominal wounds and that sort of thing, which were bedridden and couldn't be moved. However, the time came when the Germans said they had got to be moved willy-nilly, and move us they did. I was one of the last to go with my heavy cases, and we were taken by ambulance to a place called Ungen which is near Waterloo in Belgium, and there we were dumped in a school and met up with a lot of French and Belgians who were very bolshie. They didn't like us at all.

I: *Why not?*

R: I don't know. The morale of the French forces, of course, was terribly low and I think that they just felt that they had this place to themselves in their own land and didn't like to be invaded by foreigners. However, the place had one advantage in that opposite was a hospital run by the nuns and these helped a great deal, not only with the rations but looking after us; looking after us not only spiritually, but providing food and well-needed dressings, and they even took some of the serious cases into their hospital with German permission. Again we weren't there terribly long when we were moved by ambulance again to Lille in what was known as the Faculté Catholique which is part of Lille University, and we were dumped in the chapel which was an enormous building, - no facilities, no beds, nothing. So fellows who were on stretchers had to stay on stretchers. I personally slept on the stool in the organ loft, and everybody housed themselves, the medicals and nursing staff, wherever they could find a corner to sit down or lie down. The wounded were dumped in the various classrooms and administrative rooms, but it took many days before any beds appeared and then they were very few. But before that they did produce some straw. The conditions there were appalling from the point of view of the wounded because by this time the wounds had been in existence some time. As you know, those days were without antibiotics, and they weren't doing very well. In fact, the only ones that did well were those full of maggots, which cleaned up all the bad tissue. I heard later that as a result of these experiences with maggots, they developed a maggot farm somewhere in the UK and put the eggs, fly eggs, into wounds to help heal them.

I: *Do the maggots have any harmful effects?*

R: Nope! Not at all! Again, one or two advantages there. The German guards were pretty lax and anybody who felt like escaping could certainly open the door, go out into the street and he was amongst so-called allies, and quite a number of people did disappear quietly, although wounded. Another advantage was that again opposite, on the other side of the road, was another private hospital run by nuns. I think it was a maternity hospital, and the Germans gave permission for us to move our serious cases into this hospital where we posted one of our more experienced medical officers to look after them day and night. And I with others went across daily to use their operating theatre and try and improve the conditions of the patients we had. But by this stage these were getting quite serious and we had a lot of deaths, from blood poisoning really, and the septic wounds for which there was no real cure.

Finally, we were evacuated from this chapel by ambulance to the main railway station where we were put on official and proper German hospital trains which were very good, very efficient, with very efficient German staff, and splendid accommodation which is the first time we'd seen any bit of luxury for weeks and months, - not so much from the personnel point of view, but from the wounded. So there were two trains, well, the two parts of the train. The least severely disabled patients were put in one part of the train and all the bed cases in another. It so happened that I was in charge of all the bed cases, while a colleague of mine was in charge of the less severe ones. But, when we got going by train overnight, we landed up eventually at a place called Hildburghausen (near Kassel) which was in Thuringia, and the less severely wounded were disembarked to be taken to another place where they could live.

I: *Did this camp have a number to it?*

R: I didn't know what it was at that stage. It was part of the 9C area we found later. I think its number was 1251, I could check that later on. At the last minute, when my colleague was going off with these less severely wounded in the ambulances, the orders were reversed. I was ordered to go with them and the other chap to take over my patients, about which he knew absolutely nothing, and in spite of appeals to common sense, the Germans insisted I went and they were quite nasty about it. I never knew what was behind that, but you had to do what you were told. We landed up in a place like Hellingly, a mental hospital, in which two buildings had been set aside, about a mile apart, surrounded by barbed wire, but there were beds. We had to split our convoy up again into two parts, those that needed surgical attention which went into the building I went to, and those who didn't need a great deal of attention and could be looked after by duty medical officers, who didn't need to do any surgery. We stayed here I think for about two years, and while it was reasonably comfortable and we had rations and a bed to sleep in, and it was reasonably warm in winter, we were completely bottled up, with a guard over us all the time. To go from one building to another for a consultation or what have you, we had to be surrounded by guards. I refused to accept parole as a matter of principle and we had to force our way on the German mind to say that we had got to move between one building and another. Then we demanded to have some exercise, and eventually this was allowed. Anywhere you went outside the wall was under guard, rifles, bayonets, bombs in their belts. The patients were never allowed to go out, outside the wire for exercise, only the medical staff of whatever rank. I think during that time we were visited by the International Red Cross, but I can't really remember when, because we did have some patients who were, I considered, unfit for further service, and under the Geneva Convention should have been repatriated, like amputees, of which we had a large number. Repatriation, of course, as you know, was attempted earlier in the war when they were all collected at Rouen, but this fell through and they were all brought back to where they came from. Several made their escape during that time. Eventually, in about 1942, without apparent reason as far as I could see, I was suddenly told to pack and move out next morning for an unknown destination.

I: *Was this in summer or winter?*

I think it was March. Cold, yes. Anyway, I was allowed to take two of my staff with me to act as batmen and carry my valise and so on. We set off with an armed guard and were put on a train. I remember sleeping the night in the main railway station on my valise in the main part of the assembly part of the station, which was filled with refugees, all lying on the floor. I don't know what they were doing; I think they were keeping warm.

I: *Where had they come from, do you think?*

R: I have no idea because I wasn't allowed to talk to them. I tried but didn't get very far. And I think this was Dresden. The next day we moved on again and I landed up in this place in Silesia called Lamsdorf, which had been a prison camp since the Franco-Prussian War in the 1870s. This was an enormous camp in the Silesian Plain, which held 20,000 sick and wounded British and Commonwealth troops, but not Allies like Russians, who were in a separate camp and more or less exterminated quietly. We weren't allowed to have anything to do with them. Anyway, this was an enormous camp, hutted, with a central kitchen and a very large collection of huts which was known as the Revier, which is the equivalent of a hospital. This was staffed by a large number of medical officers, some of major's rank who had been specialists in their own line in civil life, and this included Commonwealth people from New Zealand and Australia, as an example. I was taken to see the camp commander who was a Captain in the German Navy, whom I found a reasonably pleasant individual who refused to use the Nazi salute and was obviously merely doing a job. But as I later found, all organization was controlled by the Abwehr, which is the security side of the forces. So, he asked me about myself, and why I was here, and I told him I didn't know but that I wanted to work as I was a surgeon. He said he'd got lots of work there and had me taken out of the camp by a roundabout route to another set of buildings which is known as the Lazarett, after the German for 'hospital'. This was in its own boundaries of barbed wire, with its own set of guards but only a few yards apart. But you had to walk about a mile and a half to get from one main gate to the other. This was like any other camp, a series of huts, one of which had been allocated for operating, one for the German administration, one for the quarters of the medical staff and several blocks, four blocks, which were bigger than the others. The first two were for surgical cases, the third one for medical cases, and the fourth one for the mentally sick. And within that confine we had free movement and ran ourselves as any other hospital. The Germans supplied the rations, the water, the electricity and the guards. I found myself again fortunate. The previous surgeon had been moved before I got there, which is the German custom, and so I had no contact with what he'd been doing before me. He had a good staff of senior medical officers who were mostly consultants in civil life, a large number of whom I knew, because they had been in the Territorial Army with me, and some had even trained at my medical school, St Thomas', with me. And they were a very good and experienced crowd. But the first impression was that they were terribly pleased to see me, not because of myself but because I was one rank senior. There were lots of majors and a bit of, I think, petty squabbling went on as who was senior to whom, and so that relieved their problem straightaway. I was told in no uncertain terms, 'You're in charge now. Good luck!' I had then to inspect the camp and find out what was going on, how to work, who to approach, where everything came from: food, water, fuel and light, medical equipment and so on. We had quite a pleasant elderly German major in charge with his personal staff of sergeant-majors and people of the German medical forces. And, obviously, this had been going on for some years before I got there and they were all on working terms with each other. And this went on. I always found myself the only surgeon wherever I went, that is, the only trained surgeon. If I wanted help, I had to try and get them from elsewhere which sometimes happened. Lots of duty medical officers, good anaesthetists, radiologists, you name it. And this went on 'till 1945 when the Russians advanced, and they advanced beyond us, from east to west. The main camp was evacuated and they made [us] forced march to the west, and as you know there were terrible conditions of snow and ice in that winter. Large numbers perished on this march, including some of my personal doctors I knew. We woke up one morning to find our German guards had gone. We had a large stock of Red Cross parcels which were under German guard originally, so we had food. As we were in the middle of a forest, we went out the forest and cut our timber and we put up notices in Russian, telling the Russians who we were, and would they come and rescue us.

I: *You had Russian speakers?*

R: Had some. In a camp that size there's somebody who knows everything. But the Russians never appeared. I must say, I never took my trousers or my boots off for a long time in view of what might happen, because tank battles were obviously going on quite close outside the camp. But as you know, the Russians eventually withdrew again east of the Oder/Neisse Line - that being a river and a town, and we woke up one morning to find the Jerries were back. By Jerries, I mean goons or Germans. This was a different kettle of fish because these were first-line troops, SS; they were unpleasant; very trigger happy.

I: *What way unpleasant?*

R: Shouting orders to the tune that we were to be evacuated by train at once. I tried to make them realize that a lot of the patients were basically immoveable, very ill, splinted, everything else, but they took no notice of that and they produced two trains; they were only cattle trucks, and dirty at that. They filled the first train up with the least serious cases that we could muster. We did the choosing as far as possible, hoping that they'd leave the remainder, and my surgical colleague, Major Lauste of Brighton, went off in that train. I never really knew what happened to it. I know they landed up safely in a western area of Germany and I've met Major Lauste since.

But he again was taken away from his patients and had something else to do. Next day, the second train was loaded at bayonet point, more or less, and everybody was evacuated and I was the last to leave. We had a truck to ourselves, a cattle truck for the medical staff. We tried to get them a medical member of the staff in each truck but there were far too many trucks for the number of staff we had anyway, and this was frowned upon, and we were more or less forced into the first truck behind the engine, - doctors, nurses, the lot. And as you can imagine 50 army officers in one truck is pretty crowded and disease was rife. They only stopped very occasionally. I had to bully the Germans to let the chaps out of their trucks and sometimes they wouldn't do it at all. So there were a lot of bowel disorders and the trucks were a bit of a shambles. When they entered the trucks they had accrued some hard rations, all that was available, and the Germans didn't produce any more, nor water. I can only remember getting out of my truck on one occasion and we pinched some hot water from the engine driver to make tea, but I think that gave a lot of people more tummy trouble! However, eventually we landed up at a place call Memmingen, in Bavaria, where there was already a Stalag, 7-C, filled with Allies, - not British, but Serbians, Croats, French, Belgians, Palestinians and a few Russians. The camp was appalling; it was filthy, muddy, cold, lacked food and proper water supplies and the prisoners were really in a terrible state.

I: *Which was about March, was it?*

R: Yeah. However, you know what the British Tommy is. He soon took over, made the Germans realize that the war was ending and they had better behave or else, and then, in a matter of days, this camp was a different place; it was cheerful. The chaps took charge of all these unfortunate patients, - mostly, frostbite people because whoever and wherever they were kept, they'd been made to march without boots to stop them escaping, and even I had to do amputations. I think the only reason we got to this place Memmingen was because the weather was so appalling, with blizzards, that the Air Force couldn't fly. They were bombing the railways. Everything was bombed; all the stations we went through were flattened. And between the cracks in the wood every now and again, we could see an airplane with the roundels on, which we took to be the RAF. They didn't know we were POWs. It might have been anybody. So I think we were lucky. Anyway, this went on in the new camp, until one day we heard gunfire and then heavier fire, which was obviously from artillery, and it seemed that the two forces were on either side of the camp, which was on a hill. We had one building, which we used as an operating theatre, which had more than one storey. And we managed to get up into the roof of this and find a window we could look out of and watch this tank battle going on, which was really quite exciting.

I: *What happened in it?*

R   Well, the Allies won. The Americans won. The Jerries retired and we could see lots of white flags going up on the houses round about, and they spared the town of Memmingen; they didn't touch it or shoot it up at all. The next morning, tanks arrived. They pushed the gates down. Somebody rushed and told me because I was still in the theatre, I think, and I rushed down to the gates as soon as I could and met the Captain in charge of the tanks, and put my official version to him. So he locked all the Jerries up and we took over and then they went on, leaving a liaison officer.

I: *Had any of the German guards fled?*

R: Can't answer that because by the time I got to the main gate, they certainly weren't there. I think they hadn't fled because they got nowhere to fly to. I think they were all locked up, put in their own commanditure. And then they started complaining, that they had nowhere to sleep etc. So they were told where they got off there, and how we'd been treated in the past and they could lump it for a bit! Well, the blizzards went on. The airfield, which had been wrecked by the RAF and Americans, was close by the town. I went and had a look at it. It had huge craters of a size that you could get two or three buses in them. But they got working parties on this, somebody did, I presume the Americans; they filled up the craters and got the runways working but they couldn't evacuate us all until the 26th of April, I think it was. No. No, 26th of April was the day we were released by the Americans. It was the 6th of May, I think, when we eventually got a message to say the RAF were coming to land on the airfield and evacuate us, which they did.

In the meanwhile, we had a British liaison officer from the Army posted to us, and we were actually receiving fresh casualties from the battle front. After we were evacuated, they went on using it. The day came when I was the last Britisher to leave the camp and go down to the airfield, and I was the last one, like the captain of the ship, to board the last airplane and we went off and finished up in Rheims. It was a big American-organized camp for everybody, including prisoners-of-war, I think. And next day, I was called on the blower and told to report to a certain place in the camp at a certain time and I was then taken back to the airfield and put on a plane. We landed up at Dunsfold, in Surrey, which I recognized, though there were no signposts around. And from there we were taken to a camp of some sort for people being returned to the country, where we de-loused and refitted and eventually were allowed to go home.

I: *What kind of effect do you think this experience, these POW experiences, had on the rest of your life?*

R: Well, it's very difficult to answer that one. I don't regard it as five years wasted life because I was doing a useful job, helping other human beings to survive and overcome misery, apart from illness and wounds. And as for being a consultant-surgeon, I suppose it gave me added confidence in what one could and could not do. As regards private life afterwards, I don't think it affected it one way or another very much. I really can't think of anything outstanding that has affected me in any particular way.

I: *I was asking you earlier about the prospects
        of the people that you operated on in POW
        camps as compared to their prospects if
        they'd have been in normal life. Can you
        repeat to me what you were telling me in
        answer to that earlier?*

R: Well, if you had an illness or injury that you had
        in non-war conditions, then I think your chances
        weren't altered very much in this way. As long as
        you had somebody to give an anaesthetic for an
        operation and the material for the anaesthetic,
        then surgery is surgery wherever it's done, and
        in those days there were no antibiotics; there
        was only M&B, or sulphaniamide. And if
        somebody in prison life had acute appendix, if it
        was diagnosed, then taking it out under those
        conditions was no worse than taking it out in civil
        conditions, the difference probably being the
        nursing care afterwards, and the rations. If you
        were on their level, in-bed rations, then you took
        longer to recover. Most of the prisoners, of
        course, were of a young age group, but even
        those were liable to have a cancer, and this in
        fact did occur and I had to remove a stomach or
        a bowel in prison life because the alternative
        would have been certain death and a pretty
        unpleasant lingering one. These people under
        my care did very well in spite of the prison
        conditions. We were troubled in certain areas
        such as plaster of paris for the results of war
        wounds which hadn't healed, and there were
        broken bones and accidents in the camp or
        working parties. We ran out of plaster of paris
        which was all captured material, and there was
        no means other than the old fashioned way of

putting a bit of wood or walking stick or something to hold the fractures in place. On this particular problem, we partly solved it by persuading the Germans to buy us a cask of household building plaster such as you put on walls. Then we had to experiment with this because it made a plaster that set hard eventually but not very quickly and it wasn't workable like that. So we experimented with cutting up the string that came round Red Cross parcels and trying to hold the remains of our bandages, anything you could think of that could be incorporated in this plaster to make it more solid with less weight, but it didn't work very well. We just had to put it on. They had to stay still for a long time while it set and it was terribly heavy to carry around. And that was a problem we never really got over in my camp.

I: **What about the tools that you had for the job?**

R: Well, when we were captured and went back to our original hospital area at Camiers, what we had was then still being used by the people remaining and they had several spare suits of equipment to cope with. And when they started to move, the Germans said, 'Oh, everything's prepared for you where you're going, you needn't take anything'. Fortunately, none of us believed it, and we stuffed our pockets with anything we could think of, including a pair of scissors - which is the most useful thing to have anywhere. I still have a pair of 9" scissors which I carried from that day. I'm still using them at home now, with the arrow of the War

Department. But otherwise the Jerries said, 'Oh, no, everything's going to be fine. Everything is there already for you', which is a lot of nonsense and we got caught out the very first time and never believed them afterwards. But in Silesia, where they had this Lazarett, they found some captured British equipment and they supplemented it with their own German field equipment. Very limited, but you don't need a great deal of equipment for war surgery.

I: *What did you do for cotton?*

R: For what?

I: *For thread?*

R: Well, things like catgut soon ran out and one used just ordinary sewing cotton, which is a very fine medium for stitching. It doesn't absorb, but the reaction of the ordinary tissues to it is minimal and it doesn't normally give you a weak spot or one that is inclined to collect microbes. In fact, I carried on doing this in civil life when I came home.

I: *Did you ever do any brain operations?*

R: I can't give you the exact answer. I'm quite sure I must have done at least one but it was nothing of a major category that I personally tackled, like a brain tumour. This is where my friend Major Henderson came in. He was a renowned, world-famous brain surgeon from Leeds, Willy Henderson, and he was the leader of a head injury unit with the BEF. There was him as the head, a Major Challis was the anaesthetist in the London Hospital, a junior surgeon from Glasgow and one or two duty medical officers, and they had their own transport and equipment. But they were given the wrong directions in France when they were being evacuated and were made prisoners-of-war. Now he was asked by the Germans, as he was world-famous, to go and collaborate with other German brain surgeons and do some operating on Germans while he was still a prisoner, and this he point-blank refused and as a result he was placed in Colditz for the rest of his prison life. I was fortunate enough to persuade my camp commandant to get him out of Colditz temporarily and come and stay with me in my Silesian Stalag 8-B because we had some cases with brain damage or brain tumours, as we thought, which needed the expert to cope with, and this he did and was returned to Colditz later.

I: *Did you ever operate on any Germans?*

R: Never! On a matter of principle. The odd time it was suggested that it might be helpful if I did, I refused and so did all my staff.

I: *Did the psychological problems or conditions which POWs have to put up with interfere with their recovery from physical illness?*

R: Oh, yes, I'm quite sure of that. Some of the conditions the chaps lived in were pretty horrendous. You know, not as bad as Auschwitz, but barracks with three-tier bunks, the wood all used up for firewood to keep warm in the cold months. Sanitary conditions very, very limited and it's surprising we didn't get more trouble from it, from infection. Now you can't tell anybody that if you're living in those conditions year after year, it is not going to affect you in some way, and if you're ill, or if you have worms or a break, fracture, this is bound to affect the rate of progress. In the Lazarett, where we had one wing for psychiatric patients entirely, this was a very sad place. The people were quite demented, a lot of them, it was almost impossible to give them any treatment. A lot of them tried to escape in their delusion and they raced towards the wires and started to climb over them, and immediately they passed the little, what they called, trip wire inside the main wire, they were shot at by the sentries from the towers. And I've seen more than one chap shot at and they wouldn't even let me, as a medical officer and the senior officer present, go anywhere near him without shooting me as well.

I: *Did you get prisoners who lost the will to live?*

R: I don't know because they were in this psychiatric department, if they got as far as that, and I didn't really have the treatment of them; they had their expert psychiatrists to look after them. So I can't really answer that one.

I: *Looking back on it, what do you think are the lessons perhaps for other people should, unfortunately, such circumstances occur, that can be learned from your experiences as a surgeon in POW camps?*

R: I think from being a prisoner of war, the first thing is that with the BEF I don't think anybody was ever initiated into the fact that this might happen to him, and therefore mentally they were quite unprepared to be a prisoner. They were prepared to be shot, wounded, or even killed but not to be a prisoner. I believe later in the war, people were prepared mentally for this possible state of affairs and they knew how to behave, and to lead their lives to make it as safe as possible afterwards. I think the next thing is that if you are in a friendly country, like you were in France, escape as quickly as you can while amongst friendly people. There's always somebody who may help you. Once you get into enemy territory, it's almost impossible to get out of it, and that can be proved by the number of escapees that really got out of Germany. And, of course, in the Far East, nobody ever got out of anywhere. As regards medical officers, in theory, you're covered by the Geneva Convention if you're at war with another so-called civilized country. But even the Germans didn't behave correctly here. They obeyed the Convention to some degree but as regards repatriating medical personnel as soon as it was feasible, this didn't occur.

I: *Now, I think that we've missed something out when you were giving the chronology of your POW camp experiences. I think there was one actual camp that you missed out between Thuringia and Silesia.*

R: Yes, I can't think how this happened. It was
exciting with this broadcast but, it's a small part
really. When I was removed from
Hildburghausen, we didn't go straight to
Silesia. I found myself in a castle called
Spangenberg, and this was part of an officers'
prison camp, an Offlag. It was a beautiful old
castle on the top of a rocky prominence, with a
moat all around it. We had wild boars in it and
the old fashioned drawbridge to get in. It was
quite an experience to get there to interview
the commandant, the German commandant
there, and then be taken under the wing of the
senior British officer who was General Fortune,
who commanded the Fifty-first Highland
Division which was captured at St Valery. I was
introduced to all the top brass and then got to
know a large number of medical officers who
were there and hundreds of officers from
regiments from the British Army. This was quite
an interesting experience to talk to all these
people, not only about the war but about life in
general. It was also interesting because I didn't
know how long I was going to stay there. I
wanted to try to get out as quickly as I could.
The senior British officer and his staff asked
me if I had any hobbies, etc. And one of the
things they found out was I used to play the
piano. So I was promptly enlisted to play the
piano in my particular part of the castle. And I
was asked would I please turn up at half past
nine tomorrow morning and prepare to use it
for half an hour, and then somebody else
wanted it. Well, being the simpleton I was, I
turned up with a bit of music I found from
somewhere, relieved somebody else who said,

'Your turn, sir', and sat down and started to strum away. And to my surprise, about half way through, a hell of a commotion went on, behind me so I couldn't see, and when I did sort of stop playing and looked around, I was told, 'For God's sake, don't stop, go on making a noise'. And I realized that the red-hot stove, it being wintertime, which was keeping the place warm, was being lifted bodily aside, and underneath was the entrance to a tunnel for escaping, and out popped all sorts of characters covered in dirt and so on, and a new lot went down and the stove was put back. Half an hour later or whenever it was, my successor turned up. I went on doing this day after day. It was really quite fun. And one day I was given the chance of going down as one of the teams to see what it was like underneath, and to get my medical experience on tunnels.

I: *What were they like?*

R: Horrible! This particular tunnel never got very far because it was pure rock and they couldn't get very far at all. Anyway, I think that with the help of the senior British officer and the German commandant, and the fact that there were a lot of medical officers about doing nothing, and that I was one of the few surgeons captured, that at the end of a month, I was told to pack my bags and I was taken away, and this time I did arrive in Silesia.

I: *Can I go back to something you said when you were talking about the arrival in*

Memmingen, when you were talking about the deplorable condition that existed in that camp in Bavaria when you arrived? Because you said then, I think, quoting your words, 'You know what the British soldier is', and you described how he got things organized there. What exactly did you mean by that phrase?

R: Well, I'd seen it in the other big camps. But there's something about the British Tommy, and the equivalent in other services like the Navy and the Air Force, that seems to go down well with the world as a whole, and the worse the conditions you find yourself in, the more strength the British soldier or his equivalent seems to have. When we arrived in this place of Memmingen, the conditions as I said were appalling and immediately my chaps, as I call them, sensed this and they could see it for themselves and it wasn't a question of, 'I'm alright, Jack, we're all together; we've got a room and it's warm, etc', etc, they just went out into the camp and started getting things organized, as far as the Germans would allow, to improve it from the word go. It's difficult to put into words and I wasn't there most of the time because I was inside the operating theatre coping with the poor unfortunates with frozen feet and limbs. But I've seen it in the bigger camp as well, when the Germans were getting nasty, and the German wanted them to do something which was quite against his nature to do. And he knew if he didn't do it, he'd probably be shot or punished. If you compare it with the other nationalities, I think it's the real way of doing it because everybody except Britain was controlled by the Germans and the poor Frenchman, the Serb, the Belgian, you-name-it, who, like the Poles in particular, if they didn't toe the line without grumbling, they'd either be shot or they would say point blank, they would take it out on your family. And that made a chap think twice before he did it or didn't do it. Now, the British soldier had no compunction about this. I've seen it happen more than once. They'd tear their shirts open dramatically and say, 'Shoot me if you'd like, you can't touch my family! I won't do it!'

End of Interview

Editor's Note:

To close out an article written for the Eastbourne Medical Gazette in 1992, Tom was quoted as saying, "One of the reasons I joined the Territorial Army was to see the world; upon reflection, I would have done better with a day trip to Dieppe".

Extracts from the diary kept by LT.COL. T. HENRY WILSON, RAMC, senior British officer, Lazarett, Stalag 344, Lamsdorf, Ober Silesia, Germany

The *Lazarett* was the main hospital at *Lamsdorf* and was outside the *Lager Stalag 344.*

The *Revier* was the camp hospital inside the *Stalag 344.*

Lt. Col. T. Henry Wilson was Senior British Officer in the *Lazarett.*

Lt. Col. Crawford was the Senior British Officer in the *Revier* in the *Lager.*

RSM S. Sherriff, Royal Welch Fusiliers, was the Camp Leader in the *Lager.*

1945

January

10ᵗʰ Visit by delegation of the International Red Cross

12ᵗʰ Russians over Vistula above Cracow

15ᵗʰ Repatriation of Sick and Wounded. 200 odd from Lazarett accompanied by Capt. Gibbons and 8 Orderlies with 70 odd mental patients from Lager.

21ˢᵗ started Xmas Red Cross parcels

22ⁿᵈ British Daily Orders started. Germans tested water pump in Lazarett. Bread for 7 days. Visit by Protecting Power (Swiss). Germans ordered all equipment less 1 operating table and X-ray plant to be packed. Gunfire heard from Opeln direction.

23ʳᵈ Beds placed in cellars. RSM Sherriff and burial party removed body from Lazarett for burial. About 3,000 left in Lager. Weston arrived from Neisse with surgical limb-makers' tools.

24ᵗʰ 0810. No Germans arrived, no sentry on gate.

0830. Sentry on gate, British pickets on duty.

0900.Last German guard walked away. Squadron Leader Morris took over duty of internal security. Pickets on Wire, Gate, Food and Coal. German office entered and contact made by phone to Germans in Lager. Capt. Gorrie RAMC arrived from Straffe Lager after months of imprisonment

1030. Lager Fuhrer and Feltwebel outside wire, told we could not use telephone but two postens would return for liaison purposes. He said the Commandant ordered us to remain within wire. German troops had orders to shoot any POWs outside. He was told that British had own discipline and food for 7 days.

25th   **0510**. Awakened by the blowing up of 7 dumps. Posten on gate. Lights on wire still on

1200. Water and lights off. Using water pump and snow. Zahlmeister i/c Food and U/O Kitchen returned to arrange for the future. Key of gate left with British.

Lager Unteroffizier arrived and demanded key to be handed back to German posten on gate. Told the Commandant knew British had the key. 800 Canadian Red Cross parcels arrived from Lager 1.

Stretcher party arrived from Revier.

No water on, washing in pump water, drinking from snow and icicles or boiled pump water.

26th   0630. Light on, water off.

0900. Lights off, water on.

Rehearsal of getting patients into cellars.

Stabs apotheke returned, took remaining items, on leaving said "goodbye".

pm. A Russian Major (MO) living in Revier visited his patients in Block F. Told Luftwaffe personnel at aerodrome would keep lights and water on as far as possible

27th   0630. Lights on, water off. German and British refix phone in Wachestube.

2 pm. Funerals of Marine J. Marsh and Gunner B. McBeth, NZ Artillery, in Cemetery. Notices in Russian of British POW Camp made to hang on wire.

28th   No lights. No water. Snowing.

29th   Lights on, no water. Very cold. Bread for 2 days arrived

30th   Water and lights on until 0700. Food, German for 7 days, Red Cross 3-4 weeks.

31st   Distant activity all night. Air activity 6 Russian planes circled.

Sentry still on gate. Russians 68 miles from Berlin.

February

1st   No water. Russians 40 miles from Berlin. No wire lights

2nd   Air activity whole of night. Snow thawing.

3rd   Cellars flooded by thawing snow. Red Cross parcels from Lager 1.
To bed undressed for first time since onset (12 days).

4th   2 Russian planes over Lager.

5th   Red Cross food for 2 weeks. German food for 7-10 days. Bread finishes tomorrow. Civilians evacuating local villages. Burial of Polish Officers from Warsaw in Cemetery. To bed dressed again.

6th   Water off but pump working well. Germans investigated noises in Lazarett during night. Sentry still on gate.
1400. From Lager 1 – 700 Xmas parcels, 6 budgerigars, 1 other bird. Prepare for 2 oxen for French wagon used for transport.

7th   Artillery action Grotkau direction.

8th   Noisy night. Visit by Commandant and Lager Offizier. He wanted to know if we wanted to be moved from danger. I told him opinion was to stay. He hinted no transport anyway. He visited kitchen.

Bread arrived from Neisse by French Red Cross wagon, 155 loaves.

Gunfire intense. Slight flow of tap water.

9th   Beautiful sunny day, blue sky. Last parcels from Lager1

1030. Russian air attack on local aerodrome.

1200. Larger attack. Flak fell in Lazarett.

1400. Further attacks. 132 loaves from Neisse.

10th   Noisy night. Lights on and water on at 0830 for short time.

Food situation: BRCS parcels 2610 parcels for 600

Cigarettes 2185 rations of 25

Bulk biscuits

German food, Fair. Bread for 3-5 days

Potatoes in quantity + peas and semolina

Water on, hot wash.

11th   Quiet night, water on. Several attacks on airfield.

12th   **0830.** Attack on aerodrome, 2 others later.

1500. Visit by Chefartz Spu..x x asking for

return of lying and sitting cases if transport becomes available.

13th Few attacks on aerodrome. Coal being used too quickly, trees to be used for fires. More bread arrives

14th Awakened by heavy gunfire, some near at hand. Funeral party as usual.

15th American pilot shot down and landed nearby. Taken to aerodrome.

16th Visit by Kommandant Grossner? regarding coal and potatoes.

1530. Message from SBO in Lager with information from Commandant that the Protecting Power have asked for us to be moved to a safer area, prepare to move by packing essentials; those who can may have to walk to station, the laying being taken by French Red Cross lorry.

Preparations put in hand at once. Breslau surrounded.

17th Water off. 6 Russian patients ordered by Germans to Stalag enroute for Russian Camp Letter to SBO expressing points why it is better to stay here than to move.

Missile through roof of Block VI, another

struck McCrae's shutter.

18th Message from SBO Lager, via Lager Officer, that 3 blocks in Stalag are warned to stand by to move.

19th Freezing cold, blue sky. Food, bread 2 slices per day + 3 biscuits.
1030. Visit by Commandant and his Transport Officer.
He confirmed we move after Lager, probably not before 6 days maybe 8, we shall get 24 hours notice. He believed we would have closed wagons only.
2000. Film show

20th Lager orders out for 2,000 to entrain at 0700 21st February.

21st RSM Sherriff saw the 2,000 leave by train before returning to Lager. Many of the 2,000 ordered to entrain were missing so numbers were made up from others not expecting to move.

23rd Visit the Lager and discussed with Col. Crawford the transport position. The Commandant has allowed 1,000 to cover Revier and Lazarett cases and staff. Now remains in Lager 3,300 approximately – next train will take 2,000 leaving 1,300 for third and last train. Advised to get fit patients ready. Daily return will be sent to SBO for transport position, laying, sitting, walking.

7 pm. Patient in Block VI reported missing, originally admitted as mental patient. Not found by 2300. Sentries and stag warned.

24th Missing patient not found, Commandant and SBO informed.

25th Commandant and Lager Officer visit Lazarett regarding missing patient.

26th During past week have systematically visited all sections of the hospital. All in good shape.

27th Sudden visit by Oberartz Spr... and another Oberartz who vetted all patients for transport, they made only 58 lying, 29 fit to march and 2554 sitting cases. Missing patient found in Lager and returned to Mental Block. Sick from Neisse Arbeit Kommandant said to be in Lager, rest on march.

28th Conference with Commandant re transport for Revier and Lazarett patients and 2 staff per wagon expected on 1.3.45. Only sick to travel. Expected all medical staff and sitting sick in Lager will follow later. Destination unknown, duration uncertain. Arrangements made to move at 0900 on 1.3.45.

March

1ˢᵗ No news of move.
1200. Prepare to move pm, later cancelled.
1300. Loading of baggage on train completed for Revier and Lazarett by 1600 hrs.
1400. Burial in cemetery. RSM Sherriff's party from Lager.
Patients again warned to move at 0800 on 2.3.45.
2 visits by Commandant to discuss move and permission given for staff to stay here 2 days after patients go.

2ⁿᵈ **0730.** Wagons turn up ½ hour early. All patients evacuated by 1000. 300 odd marched to station. All cattle trucks.

3ʳᵈ **0930.** Sudden order to evacuate hospital at 1200.
1200. Paraded – fell out at 1220 in snow storm.
1240. started to walk out to Annahof station.
Train 41 wagons, 3 for Germans, 38 for prisoners at 40 per truck. Total 1520, 168 from Lazarett, remainder from Lager. All wagons shut up at dusk.
2005. Engine joined up

2100. Train started from *Annahof.*
2230. Stop at *Neisse.*

4th First stop for sanitary arrangements. Dental Officer extracted tooth.

5th *Prague,* conditions bad, diarrhoea and vomiting throughout train. Medical officers included.
Only three things the Germans had to do. Food, Water, and Sanitation. Food given out before we started; water, the troops getting what water they can; sanitation if and when the Germans allowed the troops out. The whole train had D & V, self included. Snowing hard.

6th **0730.** *Pilsen.*
Whole train allowed out. Minor operations performed. Many sick throughout train.
1520. Martenberg. Medical officers vomiting.

7th *Regensburg*
1030. Whole train allowed out for sanitary purposes, many fainting, some washing.

8th arrived at *Memmingen Swabia.* Taken to Stalag VIIB.

Released by American Forces 26th, April 1945

Important Locations of Col T. H. Wilson
during World War II

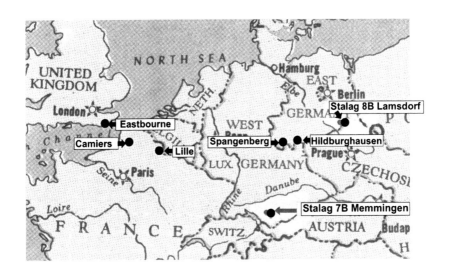

Eastbourne, UK

Camiers (20 km South of Boulogne)

Faculté Catholique of Lille University

Hildburghausen (near Cassel/Kassel) Offlag IXC

Spangenberg Schloss Offlag (for 1 month)

Lamsdorf (in Silesia), Stalag VIIIB (until January 1945)

Memmingen, (Bavaria) camp VIIB (until April 24, 1945)

Tom talking with Major Hill, of General Patton's US Army forces on *April 26, 1945*, the day the German camp Commandant surrendered to the Allied forces.

Tom waiting to board the plane that was to fly him to England on *May 8, 1945*, the day declared to be VE Day (Victory in Europe).

Editor's Note: Once the Memmingen camp Stalag VIIB had been relieved by the US Army forces, the 3936 PoW's, of British, American, French and Russian nationalities, still had to remain in camp for processing of paperwork and medical examinations before being repatriated home.

Meanwhile in a wonderful exhibition of humanity, many local citizens of Memmingen opened their doors to some of the PoW's for food, hospitality and socializing. As a result, many friendships were made, some of which have apparently continued down through further generations.

On April 26, 1995, the City of Memmingen, under the direction of the Oberburgermeister Dr. Ivo Holzinger, hosted an evening reception at the Rathaus to celebrate the 50th anniversary of the PoW camp being relieved. To this reception were invited many actual PoW's who were traceable, and some local citizen families who had socialized with them in 1945.

Copies of the book "Memmingen im Krieg" were handed out, and one copy was inscribed and signed by Dr. Holzinger and sent to Tom.

In October 2009, my German born wife Christa and I were vacationing in Austria and Germany, and we realized that we would be about an hour's drive from Memmingen. Through a family member of Christa, we made an attempt to see if we could visit the Rathaus - perhaps even to meet the current Oberburgermeister. It transpired that Dr. Ivo Holzinger was still the Oberburgermeister, and he graciously invited Christa and I to a reception at the Rathaus, with a PR representative present to record and photograph the event, and a glass of champagne offered to welcome us. A description of the event appeared in the local paper, and it was also posted on the City of Memmingen website. What class!

The Editor would like to thank the *Oberburgermeister of the City of Memmingen* for permission to use this photograph taken at City Hall during our reception.

Post-War Life

Eventually we returned to Britain on VE Day, 8th May 1945. I was given two months leave on double rations as we were pretty under-weight, and I wrote reports on everything that had happened over five years and particularly on the medical officers and the key medical staff. I was interviewed at the War Office and by MI5, and eventually l was asked to appear at one of the boards to decide my future. I was told I would be earmarked for the Far East. At this stage, I pointed out that I was completely out of date as regards surgical procedures and did not know anything about the new antibiotic, which was penicillin, and I thought I ought to be re-educated before being posted anywhere. This unpleasant and relatively junior medical officer didn't see this at all and I said 'Well, isn't there any alternative?' and he said 'Yes, you could be demobilized on your age and service group' which was a low number like No 6, and so I told him flatly that if that was the way he was going to treat me and others like me, I would opt for demobilization, which eventually happened, and I returned to Eastbourne to carry on my civilian work.

Not long after the war finished, it was decided to establish a territorial medical unit in Eastbourne to be known as the 4th (Eastern) Casualty Clearing Station, RAMC/TA. I was approached by the ADMS in the area as to whether I could consider becoming its commanding officer with the rank of Lt Colonel, which I immediately accepted. I commanded this unit for about seven years because although three years is the usual tenure for a command, nobody wanted to take it on as they hadn't the time to do so. During this time, we recruited some good medical officers from the Sussex area but hardly any from Eastbourne, and we also recruited a large number of personnel to be trained in the duties of a Casualty Clearing Station. Most of our yearly camps were spent in the Shorncliffe area and were very happy times indeed.

Finally my Major, who lived at Bexhill, agreed to take over the command and I was posted to supernumery and made a Brevet Colonel. About that time, the Reserve Army was being expanded and in particular, the Army Emergency Reserve, which used to be known as the Supplementary Reserve, and this is senior in position to the Territorial Army. I was offered a command of a General Hospital, No. 23, in this AER, with headquarters at the Headquarters of the RAMC at Ash Vale, near Aldershot, Hampshire. These were good units because they were recruited from people like myself who wanted to do national service and had previous experience, most of them, and trained for two weeks every year ready for mobilization. I did this for many years until the politicians decided to scrap a large part of all three services including the Reserves, and at last I was put on the shelf, as a reservist who could be recalled if necessary.

That is the end of my service career in brief.

When I was eventually repatriated, I did not know where the family was because we had been out of touch for the last nine months of the war, and by then it was May 1945. So I had to get the British Red Cross to find out where they were, and it was confirmed that they were still in Harpenden. They made contact for me, telling them that I was safely home, and we arranged to meet the next day.

On the day of my return, which was VE Day, 8th May 1945, we landed at an airfield called Dunsfold, close to Guildford. Of course all the signposts had been removed, but from the back of the lorry on which I was travelling, I recognized the terrain. We landed up at an Army establishment somewhere in the Guildford area, where I was interviewed for a long time that night.

Next morning I was given a voucher for a railway journey to Victoria and ration cards with double rations for I think six weeks. I was taken by lorry to the station and arrived in London, I think at Waterloo, where Olive was waiting for me at the end of the platform. As you can imagine it was a great moment in both our lives, and from there we took a taxi to

The Family, *(l to r)* Anthea, Olive, Sandra, Tom, Crichton
in the garden of 6 Carlisle Road, in Eastbourne, approx. 1950.

Websters in Dover Street where other members of Olive's family were gathered, as well as all of the staff. I have a very hazy recollection of that day, but finally we moved to Golders Green where I settled in for a few days. Soon of course I visited my parents in Chevening Road who were delighted to see me and I to see them, because my mother and father had been bombed out twice, and my father had had an emergency operation for a perforated peptic ulcer. I was glad to see them so well in spite of their trials and tribulations, and low rations.

Some time after that we must have gone to Harpenden where I have a vivid recollection of Anthea, who was then about eleven years old, rushing down the platform as I got out of the train and throwing herself into my arms, obviously delighted to see me, although she couldn't have remembered very much about me. At some time we must have made the journey to Hellingly Hospital because the Rollistons, with whom I had been billeted before going to France, had been terribly kind to the family and had housed my Rover car, putting it up on blocks for the whole of the war, as well as quite a bit of the clothing which the family had not taken with them to Harpenden. They seemed delighted to see us both and to my surprise I found that Mr. Rolliston had got the car re-organized with a new battery, had had it tested, and it was ready for driving on the road, and back we went to Harpenden.

The next stage I can remember is that time we went down to Wellington, in Somerset, because young Crichton, then eight, had gone to an Eastbourne prep school called Chelmsford Hall, and this had been evacuated to Wellington in Somerset. So we travelled down on our petrol ration and eventually found the school, and we were welcomed by the headmaster, Colonel Stevens, and his family. Crichton was allowed out with us for the rest of the day and we went out and had lunch at, I think, the Squirrel Inn. Crichton did not know me at all because he was very young when I left for the war, and while he knew his mother pretty well, I was a stranger to him, and it was sad on that day because he really didn't want to know me. This I can well understand - I was a stranger in his life and he had to start realizing that he not only had a mother but also a father.

(Editor's Note: It is my recollection that I was informed by Colonel Stevens of their impending arrival, and I was taken to the railway station (Taunton?) to meet their train. I believe that I ran down the platform and jumped into the arms of – my mother!)

So we returned him to the school, and we didn't meet up again of course until the end of the summer term, when he somehow got back to Harpenden. During this time I still had to wear my uniform because I hadn't any other clothes - they were all in store. But this didn't seem to bother anyone because the rest of the world was still in uniform as well.

I had to go up to visit the various Departments of the War Office in London at odd times and in the meantime I tried to scribble out a resumé of my experiences as a prisoner-of-war, including the work we did in the battle of Boulogne, and recommending as many personnel under my care as I thought fit for some award. This all had to be done in longhand on any bits of paper I could find, and I eventually delivered it to the War Office. I was pleased to find that most of my recommendations were accepted in due course and the personnel were awarded various branches of Orders of the British Empire.

(Editor's Note: As of December 20, 1945 he was himself appointed as an Additional Officer of the Military Division of the Order of the British Empire (OBE). He was rather disappointed that he was not invited to Buckingham Palace for the Investiture, but received his medal by post.)

So the next stage now was to get back to civil life and I took a journey to Eastbourne and saw my partners, Turner and Churcher, who had been active throughout the war in Eastbourne as two of the few doctors allowed to remain, and it was agreed that I should return as soon as possible and take up my duties as the third partner in the practice on an equal third basis.

So down I drove one day in my Rover with some spare clothing - civilian clothing this time - and I was put up at one stage by a friend of mine called Leonard

Official certificate of the appointment of Tom as an *Additional Officer of the Military Division of the Order of the British Empire.*

George R.I.

George the Sixth by the Grace of God of Great Britain, Ireland and the British Dominions beyond the Seas, King Defender of the Faith, Emperor of India and Sovereign of the Most Excellent Order of the British Empire to Our trusty and well-beloved Thomas Henry Wilson Esquire Fellow of the Royal College of Surgeons Lieutenant Colonel in Our Royal Army Medical Corps **Greeting**

Whereas We have thought fit to nominate and appoint you to be an Additional Officer of the Military Division of Our said Most Excellent Order of the British Empire We do by these presents grant unto you the Dignity of an Additional Officer of Our said Order and hereby authorize you to have hold and enjoy the said Dignity and Rank of an Additional Officer of Our aforesaid Order together with all and singular the privileges thereunto belonging or appertaining

Given at Our Court at Saint James under Our Sign Manual and the Seal of Our said Order this Twentieth day of December 1945 in the Tenth year of Our Reign

By the Sovereign's Command

Grant of the dignity of an Additional Officer of the Military Division of the Order of the British Empire to Lieutenant Colonel Thomas Henry Wilson, M.B. F.R.C.S. R.A.M.C.

Earp, who ran Oakden's Estate Agents of Eastbourne. He himself had been away in the RAF and was now demobilized also, and he lived in a delightful house called Ravensworth in Carlisle Road, just a little up the hill from Eastbourne College. I stayed there a few weeks and that was a pleasant interlude, being well looked after by his wife and cheered up by two delightful girls. All this time I was using my partners' consulting rooms to see various patients, and the car to get around visiting their homes.

Leonard Earp helped me greatly in trying to find a house, but there weren't many appropriate houses in Eastbourne at that time in 1945, because a lot of them were still occupied by the military, and those that had been emptied needed a lot of repair work done to make them habitable. Eventually there was a house in Carlisle Road which seemed reasonable, but I didn't really like it because it had many steps up to the front door and this wasn't good for patients who were disabled, and it didn't compare with the house which I had had pre-war, called Bendemeer. However, it was Hobson's choice, and I got a surveyor to make sure it was all right and habitable, and this he did. But on one of the early occasions when I stepped through the front door myself, I put my foot through the floorboards which were obviously rotten. So I sacked the surveyor and refused to pay his fee as he had made a very bad report on my case. So I had to start all over again.

Before I went to war, Eastbourne College authorities had said of course I could come back to Bendemeer after the war, but this was impossible because the Navy had taken it over for the whole of the war and they were still in residence, and unlikely to move out in a hurry. So I had to look further afield.

I was again lucky that Leonard Earp was on my side because he came to me and said there was a nice house, a suitable size and a pleasant place, in Carlisle Road, No 6 in fact, which was next door to Powell House, which was part of Eastbourne College, where they housed the day boys of the College. This house, No 6, had already been acquired by a nursing sister called Miss Hawkins, whom I knew from pre-war days when she had a nursing home in another part of the town. She had acquired this No 6 as she thought of opening it as a new nursing home post-war. However, somehow the Duke of Devonshire's agent, I think it was, refused to allow it to be used as a nursing home.

6 Carlisle Road

The house had a small driveway with two entrances, one on Grassington Road, and the other on Carlisle Road, which was presumably previously used for carriage and horses to go in and out. But the former exit had been bricked in for safety reasons, now that there were no longer horses and carriages. So you went in the drive and immediately in front was a double-fronted bow-windowed house with a porch outside the front door. There were two storeys above. On entering the front door you were in a medium-sized entrance hall and if you went straight ahead, you went down three stairs to a door which opened into the garden. To the left of the hall there was a big bay-windowed room which I used as a lounge and out of which there was a door on the Westside into a lean-to and a large greenhouse. The next door on the left of the hall led to a smaller room which I used as a dining room and waiting room, and outside this second door was the first flight of stairs going up to a half landing and then on again. On this half landing there was a toilet, and there was also another toilet immediately below it by the door to the garden - all very convenient. To the right of the hall there was a little passage to the kitchen and immediately to the right was the door into a big bay-windowed room which I used as my consulting room. Opposite that there was the butler's pantry which was all sealed up with iron bars over the window. Further down the corridor there was a huge kitchen and outside that a door to the outside, and a flight of stairs going up to the next floor; in other words, the servants' stairway.

Through the kitchen, which had an Aga cooker, you went down a step into the scullery, where the main boiler was for heating the water, and beyond that a second small room through which you went out another door into the garden.

As you went in the drive before getting to the front door, there was the bow window of the consulting room but to the right of that there was a fitted aviary which was still in existence including its own bath and little bars and a fountain. I eventually had this cleaned out and in the space between the aviary and the neighbouring wall of Powell House I had a single-car garage built. The original garage had been in the north end of the garden a long way from the house and this had had a direct hit by a German bomb and no longer existed. On going up the main stairs there was a half landing, then more stairs leading into quite a nice little hall or landing. On this first floor there were five bedrooms. Overlooking the front of the house, onto Carlisle Road, were a main bedroom and dressing room, a bathroom, and another bedroom. Overlooking the garden at the back of the house were two bedrooms, and there was another bedroom overlooking Grassington Road on the side of the house.

The main stairway went on up another flight to another landing and two good bedrooms, and two smaller bedrooms, off one of which was a room containing the hot and cold water tanks. The landing on the first floor was big enough and long enough for the family to play cricket there, and the fast bowlers had to come up the 'servants' stairs before delivering the ball. Eventually we got the furniture out of store and settled it round the various rooms in the house and finally the family all came down from

Harpenden, and we took up residence. It was a happy house and eventually we managed to get hold of a parlour maid to join up with the cook whom we had had pre-war and who was with the family all the time at Harpenden. At that stage the Butler found himself another job.

I used to see my patients for two surgeries a day. There were not many of those, they were mostly on Lloyd George's National Health panel at that time. I think that there were only 400 in all which I took over from Dr. Turner. So not many appeared at any one surgery. Of course, in addition, one had private patients and the fees in those days were quite small, even as low as five shillings to come to the surgery, and seven shillings and sixpence to be paid a house visit. In my particular case, I was surgeon to the Eastbourne voluntary hospital, the Princess Alice Hospital, and although that was a voluntary honorary appointment, I did have private patients to be operated upon in the nursing homes and of course, this brought in increased fees.

During the next few years, the practice increased and of course the receipts increased too, so that by the time the National Health Service started in 1948, we had a good practice of three people, with a good income.

At this time, the Government decided that to enter the Health Service as Medical Officers you could remain in practice or become a consultant, and if you wished to become a consultant or were already a consultant, if you continued to have a practice as well, then you couldn't have more than four sessions of hospital work. In our case the practice decided to split amicably. Dr. Turner decided he would cease practising altogether as he was no longer young. Dr. Churcher and I decided to part amicably as partners, and he carried on his practice with four sessions as a consultant physician. I gave up the practice altogether and was allowed to do full-time surgical work in the hospitals but elected to be what was called 'maximum part-time', in other words nine out of a possible eleven sessions a week, which allowed one time to do private practice as a surgical specialty.

The Government decided to buy out all practices and so in the case of Dr Turner he was paid in full. In the case of Dr Churcher, he wasn't paid at all, and he couldn't get his money for his practice until either he could show hardship or he gave up practice entirely. In my case, as I had given up practice entirely, I would be paid in full. The terms of payment were not good and that was one of the reasons why most doctors at that time did not wish to join the Health Service, purely because of the financial arrangements, and not because they disliked the idea of the Health Service, which I personally approved of. So the decision as to whether you could become a consultant or not rested with the medical profession who had its own headquarters in London, and they decided for the whole of the United Kingdom who was eligible to be a consultant, or who was not. In the area of Eastbourne, I was the only one who was thought sufficiently well qualified and capable to be allowed to call myself a consultant surgeon in the Health Service. I might add this caused a lot of misgivings amongst my colleagues who of course fought this decision, but over quite a few years almost all of them became recognized consultants in one specialty or another. There were one or two who had been doing surgery in the hospital voluntarily who had not got the requisite qualifications although they had the experience, and they were not ever allowed to be any kind of consultant in the new Health Service.

If I remember correctly, the remuneration was pretty dismal for consultants. You started at the lowest grade at something like £3,500 a year, and over the years you would be gradually increased to a maximum for a full-time consultant surgeon position of about £4,500 per year.

Having been bought out of practice, and the practice having done well on the accountants' showing, I was paid a goodly sum which I actually don't remember except that it was sufficient to wipe out entirely the loan I had taken out in pre-war days, and added to post-war. So from that stage onwards, 1948, I didn't have a mortgage round my neck.

Post-war Medical Career in Eastbourne

(Editor's Note: Tom did not write anything about his own post-war medical career. The following should go some way towards filling that gap)

Upon returning to Eastbourne, he took up again his pre-war duties in medical practice as the third partner with Drs Turner and Churcher. He also spent a lot of time going to visit various London Hospitals to catch up on his surgical skills, and learning about new techniques and medications (e.g. penicillin).

Later he was appointed full surgeon to the Eastbourne Voluntary Hospital, the Princess Alice Hospital. He also became a Consultant Surgeon to the Leaf Hospital and St Mary's Hospital, and performed private surgical work at the Esperance Nursing Home. This private Nursing Home was staffed by medically-trained nuns, most of whom came from Ireland.

He retired from his position as Consultant Surgeon to the Eastbourne Hospitals in 1969, but continued with private consultations.

In 1985 he was invited to attend the Eastbourne Town Hall where the Mayor, Councillor Leslie Mason, on behalf of the Town Council presented him with a plaque and a citation to celebrate his services to Eastbourne for 50 years.

By coincidence one of the attendees at the presentation was the then local Liberal Democrat leader, Councillor Maurice Skilton, who had been the very first patient attended to by THW in France in 1940,

On October 15, 1986 he was admitted by Her Majesty the Queen as Officer (Brother) of the Most Venerable Order of the Hospital of St. John of Jerusalem

Chaseley
Late in 1945, he was approached by the then Mayor of Eastbourne, Alderman Miss Alice Hudson, to see if he would be interested in looking after war-paralyzed patients in a Home that was proposed to be set up in Eastbourne, This was to be a residential home for patients coming from the Stoke Mandeville Hospital run by Dr. (later Sir) Ludwig Guttman, who had made huge changes in the treatment of patients paralyzed from spinal injuries.. Dr Guttman's ideas on using water-supported therapeutic exercise, and later, other sporting activities as therapy (e, g. archery) led to international sporting competitions for paraplegics, which have since grown into the Paralympic Games.

Tom accepted the idea and was officially appointed Medical Officer to Chaseley Hospital in June 1946 after having taken a course up at Stoke Mandeville on the problems and treatment of paraplegics. He devoted much of his time and efforts to the patients there, and it was said by nurses "You had to tell him even if a resident sneezed, yet he was so approachable to both residents and staff".

He was quite proud of achieving one of the few early successes of performing an appendectomy on one of the residents. Due to the paralysis, the patients often do not feel the normal pain of such things as broken legs or appendicitis, and so diagnosis and treatment or surgery get delayed. THW had to weigh all the other puzzling symptoms, decided to operate, successfully, just before the appendix burst.

He remained Medical Officer at Chaseley until 1983, when at the age of 78, he was translated to Medical Advisor, and at that time the original part of Chaseley was named the Henry Wilson wing in an official ceremony.

He had attended the Chaseley Trustees' meetings since 1960, and from 1983 he proceeded to serve for over ten years as Chairman of the Chaseley Management Committee.

He remained very attached to Chaseley and made a point of attending there every day when in town, even *into his nineties.*

On October 28, 1996 the Chaseley Appeal was launched, coinciding with Chaseley's 50th. birthday. At a dinner that evening, the Trustees took the opportunity to present THW with a plaque and a silver tea set in honour of his 50 year association with Chaseley.

We got the house furnished and lived in and everything was working smoothly. But we had to fight to get payment for war damage, which included the destruction of the garage and ruining the garden, especially the tennis court. The house itself seemed intact. Eventually payment was agreed upon and I was paid sufficient to build the new garage, and have the garden re-landscaped and the tennis court re-laid. From then on we had a very happy outdoor life in the garden, tennis court and kitchen garden.

Another interesting thing is that the Government wouldn't allow you to spend more than £100 on repairing any property, but it was quite surprising how far £100 went in those days. At No 6, the bath had been badly stained and rusted and I was able not only to replace that with a completely new bath and taps, but to re-decorate quite a large part of the living quarters with the simple paintwork to make the house very smart. After all, in pre-war days you could buy a Morris Minor car for £99!

Anthea went to school at Ravenscroft, up on the seafront, and Crichton continued at Chelmsford Hall prep school, now returned from its war-time evacuation to Somerset, where he was captain of cricket and head boy, and then he transferred as a day pupil to Eastbourne College. Anthea remained at Ravenscroft girls' school as a day pupil until she took the old-fashioned London Matriculation examination and passed first time, which put her father in the shade as he took no less than six times to pass! So she spent her young days at No 6 Carlisle Road. When she was 18, she had to leave School and had decided a long time before that to take up nursing as a profession, and had actually been accepted to start at St Thomas' Hospital in London, where I had been a student and eventually a registrar, but she wasn't allowed to start until she was 19 plus because that was the rule in those days. So she did some time at Stonehouse Farm at Hellingly, which was owned by Mr. and Mrs Thorpe, and then later she did a job as an 'au pair' girl in Geneva with a pastor of some church.

I don't think she was particularly happy in Geneva but it filled in the time and gave her a wider experience of the world. Anthea eventually came back and did her four years training at St Thomas' Hospital, which I think she thoroughly enjoyed in spite of the fact that the rules were very strict in those days; there was no money available and they had a fairly thin time socially. But her class seemed to have a large number of delightful girls, a few of whom became very close friends, and particularly her friend Polly, and I know that they still see each other regularly.

The day came when Anthea was engaged to be married to a fellow called Giles Langton whom we as parents had not known personally but had seen him as a pupil at Eastbourne College regularly because he was tall and red-headed and was a good cricketer and rugger player. He was obviously a man to watch, though at that time we didn't know him. It so happened that Anthea's bosom pal at Ravenscroft was a nice girl called Ann Symington who lived at King's Lynn. Through the school, we got to know Ann's parents, and in fact one year we even stayed with them for a few days when we were up in the area. Ann had a 21st birthday party to which Anthea was invited from St Thomas' Hospital and while at that party she met and fell in love with this Giles Langton. So they became engaged and she was married from 6 Carlisle Road at St John's Church in St. John's Road, Eastbourne, which is very close to her school at Ravenscroft.

This marriage was quite an occasion, as you can understand, being the first in the family. Great preparations were made at 6 Carlisle Road and Mr. Prodger, who regularly cleaned our cars, was persuaded to act as chauffeur of the Bentley we had at the time and we all set off to St John's Church on 10th

January 1959. It was a delightful, bright sunny day, but terribly cold and while the service was nice and the church warm, taking the photographs outside was a chilly business, especially for the bride and bridesmaids in their beautiful but thin clothes.

We all went down to the Grand Hotel afterwards where the Director, Dick Beatty, took charge and gave us a great reception and party with refreshments. I don't remember a great deal about it except that the time passed all too quickly, talking to all the family and guests, especially the family of the bridegroom, and listening to the speeches. Finally, the bridal pair changed into their 'going away' clothes and were sent on their way to their honeymoon.

Of course this wasn't the last we saw of them as he was a farmer and had settled at a place called Little Wenham, close to Ipswich, and naturally we used to go down and see them.

When we started to live at No 6 Carlisle Road, Crichton was about nine years old and he continued to live there until we all moved house after about twenty years. At first he was a day boy at Chelmsford Hall, which was just up and across the road on the opposite corner, where they had the main school buildings, with the playing fields on the other side of the road between Carlisle Road and Granville Road. He eventually quietly grew up and didn't have a bad scholastic career, but certainly he was outstanding at sports, particularly cricket and tennis, as well as athletics, because he was above average in height for his age, as well as being slim. During his final year at Chelmsford Hall, as he was to be made head boy, we decided as parents to allow him to become a boarder, as it was not really advisable to be head boy as a day pupil.

Crichton started at Eastbourne College in the September term of the year 1950. He steadily worked his way through the various forms at the College and had a reasonably good education and acquitted himself quite well to a point that was able to enter Cambridge University at Clare College in the year 1957. He steadily grew in height and particularly during the time when he had a leg injury and had to lie up, and was not able to do anything physically for quite a long period. Eventually he reached the enormous height of 6 ft 5 inches, being slim and well built with it. This enabled him to do well at the various sports he was keen on, especially cricket and tennis. I know for a short time he played some rugby though he didn't really fancy it, and took up hockey and became quite a good player.

I can well remember coming home to lunch one day and I was told that Crichton, at the age of 15, had been pulled out of his class to take the place in the First XI cricket team of someone who had fallen sick. The following year, in the first match of the season, he scored an unbeaten century, and he acquitted himself very well thereafter. He maintained his place in the team and eventually became captain in his last year.

I don't think it has happened before and will probably never be allowed to happen again, but he became captain of cricket and the leading tennis player in the same year, and the school had to try to arrange that tennis and cricket matches did not coincide.

While he was growing up he of course had a lot of academic work to do but the school was so geared that even day boys did most of their homework in the classrooms in the College before they went home for the day, and so sometimes they didn't get home until 8, 9, or even 10 o'clock in the evening. However there were many occasions when his particular cronies used to foregather in the large kitchen of 6 Carlisle Road and there they entertained themselves aided by the family, did some cooking, and lots of eating, and I think a good time was had by all.

There was a particular group, all of the surnames beginning with 'W' - four in all, namely Wood, Weight, Wells, and Wilson, and I know this friendship has persisted up to the present day, although they are well scattered geographically.

Another part of Crichton's career at school was that he had to become a member of the College Cadet Force, and elected to be part of the Royal Air Force Section. This enabled him to obtain a flying scholarship, as had his friend Brian Meaby, by which the RAF paid for them to take pilot training and to qualify for a pilot's licence before even leaving school. I think this was quite an occasion to schoolboys.

So at the time he had to leave school in the year 1955 he was not only a qualified pilot but he had obtained a place at Clare College, Cambridge, in the hopes that he could study engineering. An interesting point is that at that time, the Master of Clare College was Sir Henry Thirkhill, who had been tutor to my two younger brothers when they had gone to Clare in the 1930s.

At this time also it was necessary for him to do his two years of National Service and this he elected to do in the RAF, and it was also decided that it would be to his advantage if he did this before he went to Cambridge. In the course of his service, Crichton went through Officer Cadet School at Kirton-in-Lindsey, Lincolnshire, and my wife, Olive, and I went up there to watch the passing-out parade of his course. With the rank of Acting Pilot Officer, he was then posted to RAF Hullavington in Wiltshire where he spent about a year in pilot training on piston-engined Provost aircraft. From there came a posting to RAF Oakington, outside Cambridge, for training on jet-engined Vampire aircraft. Unfortunately this training was disrupted by a leg injury that occurred on the hockey field, and by the time he was declared fit again, there was insufficient time remaining in his two years of service to complete training to the level of getting his 'wings'. So he was discharged a little short of the two years.

He then went up to Clare, Cambridge, (where my younger brothers Bill and Joe had gone in the late 20's to study Theology and Medicine respectively) for the usual three years and I think he had a very good and interesting life there, meeting lots of people in all walks of life, many of whom he is still in contact with. He also played a lot of sport, and found most success in tennis. He ended up in his last year as captain of the Cambridge University Grasshoppers, the 'varsity second team, and played in about half of the first team's matches, just missing out on getting a 'Blue'.

At the end of the summer of 1960, we went up to see Crichton in the graduation ceremony and were very proud to be able to go up to Cambridge where, from our reserved seats in the Senate House, we were able to see him accept his degree wearing his cap and gown. After that he found himself employment in the aircraft industry.

When we had become established as a family at No 6 Carlisle Road, some time in 1945, we decided that we would like another child and eventually this infant arrived on 3rd January 1947, being born in No 6 Carlisle Road, when we had the same midwife as we had had for Crichton's birth pre-war, and she looked after Sandra.

The new infant was a girl with red hair and eventually as the hair developed it was a most delightful colour and kind friends referred to it as titian. She was to be called Sandra and then Elizabeth, and she was christened in the Church almost opposite the house, All Saints Church in Carlisle Road.

Sandra grew up steadily without any problems and I am sure we had a nanny for her in those days, and in fact we had more than one, but not at the same time. She started at a nursery school and when old enough she too went to the girls' school on South Cliff called Ravenscroft, and completed her schooling there until she left when she was 18. She too was anxious to do nursing, but elected to get herself lined up with Dr Barnado's Institute at Tunbridge Wells, where there was a trainee school for nursery nurses. I remember taking her there in the car and seeing her established there, and that was in 1965.

I think she had a happy time there for two years and met a lot of nice girls, and in particular she became very friendly with a girl called Janet Abraham, whose parents lived in Sidmouth in Devon, and who also had a brother. It was quite obvious that she was very friendly with this girl and got to know the family and the brother Peter quite well. The natural thing happened and they became engaged and eventually married.

The curriculum at Dr Barnardo's was very wide-ranging but when they had finished they were very well qualified to deal with children and their minor ailments, not to mention with their parents, and she herself got a high grade pass similar to an honours degree.

While all this was going on, she was living with us at No 6 Carlisle Road except when she went to Dr Barnado's, where of course she was resident. But just after my elder daughter, Anthea, got married, we realized that the house was much too big for us, with the two elder children being away, and only the youngster living with us on and off, and also it was getting difficult to get and keep staff. This was a house that needed coal to be put into the Aga cooker and the hot water stove about three times a day.

So I started looking around and even talking to Eastbourne College as to whether they would be interested in buying No 6 from me as it was adjacent to their other premises. Nothing came of this for some time, and then one day the best architect in the town, Hubbard Ford, came to me and said he had heard that I was thinking of selling my property, and he might be interested. We discussed this amicably and it seemed that what he wanted to do was to pull the house down and build a block of flats, while I was much more in tune with seeing it have a good owner, and preferably Eastbourne College, to which I also had some attachment through my son and other friends. Eventually Eastbourne College became very interested and offered me £10,000 for the property but they were not in a hurry to take it over, which suited me because I needed to find somewhere else and arrange to continue my work as a consultant surgeon.

As luck would have it, I knew the mayor at the time and his wife was a sister of this chap Hubbard Ford. They were the owners of the Rustington Hotel in St John's Road, close to the sea, and more fortunate still, they had two flats, one above the other at the upper-hill end of the block, and the ground floor one was vacant. My wife and I looked over this and we thought it was delightful, and also because not only were the owners nice people, but the flat itself had a big bow fronted front room overlooking the sea at an angle. There was also a big bedroom at the back that overlooked the town, with another smaller room, and kitchen and bathroom and usual offices. It had its own back and front doors, and more importantly, had its own doorway from the hall leading straight into the hotel ground floor, and that meant that we could use the hotel dining room and did not have to do any cooking or washing up. So this was all fixed up and we agreed to move, and store all the furniture except a few pieces we wanted, and we could furnish the flat ourselves as we wanted to.

All the furniture from No 6 went into store, we kept what we wanted for the three rooms we would have, and we were very comfortable indeed. I don't think we ever cooked a meal and I don't think we ever washed up. This flat was also nice because there was a nice bedroom for Sandra and the hotel was very close to her school which was opposite on the other side of the road and she occasionally brought her friends home after school. There was a small entrance hall inside the front door, and this had curtains and was large enough to take a bed, which enabled Crichton, or anyone else for that matter, to doss down there for a few days at a time, while we could use the back door to come into the flat.

I was also fortunate in the fact that the owners gave me permission to see my patients there for consultation and even allowed me to put my professional plate on the gate. So everything was very rosy. The hotel was a big one being composed of a series of Georgian mansions, each for one family at one time, but now all lopped together into a big block to make this huge hotel. In addition the owners were practising Christians and so the day always started off with prayers, and sometimes when I had time to spare I joined in, and that way got to know a lot of the residents, many of whom were there on a permanent basis.

Altogether we stayed there I think for two years and when the time came to leave we were so happy and comfortable there, we didn't really want to move.

While we were living in this hotel I was having a

new house built. This architect, Hubbard Ford, was a very nice person and he and his staff settled down to draw up plans for the requirements we needed. I had been fortunate enough, through my old friend Leonard Earp, to find a plot on which to build, because when we wanted to move from No 6 Carlisle Road, we wanted something small and compact. But we wanted some ground, preferably with a grass tennis court, in a nice locality where I could see my patients as well. Leonard came to me one day, after several years trying to find a place to live, saying he thought he had found a spot I would appreciate, and we arranged to meet at 8.30 on a summer morning before we started our ordinary work. He wouldn't tell me where it was so it came as a surprise.

Now thereby hangs a tale, because one of the things I had done over the period was to write to the owner of a particular house in Paradise Drive, whom I did not know but whom I knew was elderly, asking him if he would consider selling his property, and to which I never got any reply. In my view sometimes elderly people merely need a push or a suggestion which they can fit in, and move out of a large property into something more suitable for their age and energy. It so happened that my friend Leonard Earp led me to the very property I had wanted.

However, it was not quite as simple as that. The elderly owner did not want to move out, but he did offer me a large plot of land – perhaps three quarters of an acre – between his house and the original master house of this area.

It was a lovely sunny morning and I was very taken with the plot. I had no hesitation in putting down my deposit of £4,500 for the ground. When I say a deposit, it was the sum payable for the plot.

So from there Hubbard Ford started drawing up plans and getting costs of putting a house on this site which was an elongated site with one end backing onto the wall of the Eastbourne Golf Club and Compton Place owned by the Duke of Devonshire, and the other end onto Paradise Drive, with about 20 yards between the two boundary sides. The ground was divided into two parts by a brick wall which, from the old plan and aerial photographs I had seen, divided the ornamental garden of the original house from the kitchen garden and orchard, and as it so happened a hard tennis court.

This hard tennis court was now derelict but could have been repaired. However the only place to site the house was at the side of the tennis court which was on the golf club side of the wall, which gave us lovely views northwards over the Downs. It was quite obvious one didn't want a school playing field outside one's living room windows, and so we decided to rip the top surface off the court and use it for the hardcore for a driveway we had to make, and then we got the experts in to put the loam on the existing foundations and returf it. So that we were actually playing tennis before we were resident in the house.

The plans proceeded and the first costings of what we wanted were half as much again as the money I had, and I said that I could only afford £11,000. That was for the house, drive and garage as distinct from the ground which I had already paid for and was freehold. So I told Hubbard Ford that at no time had he ever said I couldn't have what we had suggested for the money, in other words a five-bedroom house. I more or less told him that I wasn't going to pay his charges and would have to start again and keep it down to the right amount of money. This we did. We cut out one bedroom, shortened the house, modified the plans slightly, cut out all the frills like bay windows, gates for the drive, and you name it, and the final plans which included the fifth bedroom in the roof brought the price back to £11,000.

The house became ready and we moved in at the beginning of October 1960. We got the furniture out of store and fitted it all in, but of course we couldn't get in nearly as much as we had in the old house, and a lot of our nice possessions had to be sold off. So we had a five-bedroom house, although one of them was in the roof.

Ascot House, Paradise Drive

We called our new home Ascot House. The name was derived from the names of the family members – Anthea, Sandra, Crichton, Olive and Tom. It is a very plain, modern construction on two floors, with a roof space which can be utilized, and the floor space is exactly 1,000 sq ft. It is finished off in plaster which has been rendered with one of these modern outdoor surfaces painted in a cream colour.

As you go up the drive, which had to be specially built with an entrance into the main wall on the road, you come to a car parking spot and the house is a little further up a gentle slope to the left side, while the double garage is to the right. If you can imagine, from where you stop the car, the house is approximately an oblong with its long length in a north/south axis, and its width east/west, the north/south length being greater than the east/west one. The front door is the first thing you come to on the right-hand bottom corner of the house and you enter there into a hall from which all the ground floor rooms open up. Immediately inside the door is a cloakroom and ahead an L-shaped room which I used as my consulting room, and from the tip of the L there is another door into the cloakroom, making a self-contained suite. As you turn right round the staircase you come across two further rooms on the west side, the first one being a dining-room and the other being a lounge, and these last two rooms are connected by an open space which can be closed off with a collapsible screen. All these rooms on the ground floor have French windows which open up on to the lawn outside. At the north end of the house is the kitchen which has a little window with a serving hatch between the kitchen and the lounge. Between the kitchen and the base of the stairs is a short passage leading to the back door, on either side of which are a series of cupboards, the main one being the boiler room, and next to it the hot water tank and drying room.

You go up the stairs, which are in three flights, making 17 steps in all. On a half landing you have a beautiful shaped large window looking out east over the neighbouring property. When you get to the top of the stairs, you turn to the right, north, to come to the main bedroom which goes across the whole width of the north end of the house, and which contained large veranda-type windows on the west, a three-piece window in the centre looking northwards over the golf course and the Downs, and smaller windows high up on the wall on the east side, where there are some of the dressing cupboards and a wash basin. These windows are at shoulder height which prevents the neighbours looking in.

As you go south down the landing there are three rooms opening off, each of which is a bedroom. The most southerly one is a double room and is the only one fitted with a basin. The two middle ones are single rooms. On the southern end of the top landing there is a big bathroom with toilet and next to it, between that and the stairs, the there is a separate toilet with a wash basin.

From centre of the landing there is a pull-down stairway which enables you to get up into the roof through a large opening, and in the roof there is the cold-water tank. There are also two dormer windows, one facing south and one west, and this part has been partitioned to make an L-shaped fifth bedroom if necessary. But there are no basins, only a radiator for heating.

The heating is, or was in the first instance, oil-fired and next to the boiler room on the first floor is the reservoir hot tank. All rooms have radiators, including the hall, to keep the house warm, and they can be controlled by a main thermostat situated on the kitchen wall, or can be closed off by means of their own valve. In the main lounge there is an open grate for an ordinary coal or wood fire.

We took up residence in October 1960 and since then the modifications have been that we have changed to gas cooking and heating, and we put on a porch over the front door fairly soon after we moved in because we found in the cold winter the north-east wind bringing the snow used to come actually under the door into the hall. In 1980, that is to say about 20 years after taking up residence, we put on a sun lounge on the south end of the house with the entrance through my consulting room. This has been a marvellous addition because it has been so convenient to get in and out of the garden that way and also take advantage of the sun and the warmth. More recently still, in 1987, we built on a utility room on the east side of the house outside the kitchen door, between the kitchen windows and the front door. And this again has been a great boon because the washing machine and store cupboards can be situated there, leaving more room in the kitchen.

The storage area in the roof was fitted out by me as a quartermaster's store and most of the things which are not in daily use are stored up there. The boarded up part of the roof which makes the L-shaped bedroom with the two dormer windows makes a very nice room but, as I said, it is without any washing facilities. It makes a double bedroom which in the early years was used by the grandchildren. It was first used by my son Crichton who only came back when working near London, being there only at weekends. When he eventually left home to take a job in Montreal, Canada, it was permanently turned over for use by the grandchildren, when they used to come down in school holidays to have some time by the sea. Now they are all grown up and most of them have children of their own, but they don't come down to stay in Eastbourne, and so the top floor has rather developed into another storeroom because when Crichton moved to Canada, he couldn't and didn't take everything he owned with him and a lot of it still remains there in case he or anyone else every wants it again. The trouble is now to try and tidy up this room because, while some of the materials have been given away to various members of the family and particularly to Valerie's god-daughters, there is still a lot left and something will have to be done to clear this out soon.

Sandra was the only member of the family, apart from Olive and me, who lived in the house permanently and that was only while she was at school. After leaving school she used to come back at intervals, of course, in her holidays while she was doing her training in Tunbridge Wells, and later when she found herself employment as a children's nurse with various families.

The time came when she met Peter Abraham and then we had a splendid wedding from this house. When she decided to get married in July 1969 in high summer, we decided that the reception should be in the garden, hoping that the weather would be fine.

She was married at St. John's Church on a beautiful day and after that we all came back to Ascot House and had the reception there. As the guests came in the gate, they could walk up a short path through the wooded part of the garden on to the lower lawn. At that stage this was a lawn, although I had put in two plants of Pampas grass and this made a nice entrance coming in to the lawn from the south side working up towards the north. Just north of the Pampas grass I had had erected a tent in case of bad weather and in this tent were arranged the various refreshments and tables and chairs for people to sit down for their meal. It was a fine day and most people stayed outside, and after meeting the bride and groom they then went further up to the tennis court at the north end of the grounds, and spread themselves around while all the entertaining went on. After the usual speeches and the cutting of the cake, the bride and groom drove away to The George Hotel, by Gatwick Airport, before flying off to Ibiza for their honeymoon.

(Editor's Note: In the early 70's, Tom and Olive separated, and Olive continued to live in Eastbourne, taking a flat in the building close to the Devonshire Park Theatre. The building was better known at that time for housing the Summer Palace, a well-known Chinese restaurant. Olive's health declined, and in 1978 she was moved to a Nursing Home on Blackwater Road, ironically converted from the former home of Dr. Churcher. Olive passed away in the spring of 1979).

I used to ski regularly in January or February of each year, and always with the Combined Services Winter Sports Association or the Army Ski Association. In the year 1973 I went to Flims Waldhaus as I had done many times before, in company with my friends, Dick and Daphne Bowen, and John Marriot and his wife.

That particular year I had arranged with the Combined Services secretariat that my son, Crichton, could come and join our party at Flims and also bring another friend from Montreal, Canada, if he so desired, as I thought it was about time that Crichton skied with his father before the latter became too old to ski at all. I must say that Crichton was very enthusiastic about this and came over from Canada to join the party with us at Flims Waldhaus for a fortnight, with Mike Millard, a Montreal friend and wonderful skier, who had done much to encourage Crichton in his skiing.

Early in the fortnight the Combined Services representative, a Colonel Middleton, told me that the secretary of the Combined Services Association was coming to stay at our hotel in the course of her yearly visit to Switzerland to visit all the ski resorts at which the Combined Services Winter Sports were operating in order to make sure things were working well and to arrange the contracts for the next year. I asked the Colonel if he would be good enough to introduce me to the secretary as I wished to thank her for her additional efforts in arranging to get Crichton and his friend over under the scheme   One night when we were all at dinner, I had pointed out to me a lady, tall and slim, who I was told was this particular secretary. She joined another table of friends of mine, who happened to be two surgeons who had trained at St Thomas' with me, though l had been senior to them, one being John Williams, a surgeon at Bury St Edmunds and the other a Colonel Birdwood who had been in the Indian Medical Services and was now retired and living at Bideford in Devon.

After the meal I was introduced to this charming lady and that was the first time I met Miss Valerie Storey. I thanked her for arranging to get Crichton and his friend over to join us and introduced her to them. Later on we all went down to the hotel ballroom, and during the course of the evening I asked her to dance with me. It turned out to be a Viennese waltz and I found she was an excellent dancer, and we made a good dancing couple.

The following night there was a special candlelight gala dinner in the main dining room of the hotel where all the food was brought in on dishes held aloft by all the various chefs, and an excellent dinner was had by all. As the British were in the minority in the hotel as a whole, there being mostly Swiss and also other nationals, it was arranged somehow that the two prominent British groups, mainly ours and Col Birdwood's group, should be adjacent, and that made it easier for us to talk to each other. In the course of the evening I naturally asked Valerie to dance with me again. From that time onwards I saw her several times during our holiday and, when she eventually departed with Col Middleton, to travel by car back to

Britain, I was astonished to find that I had been paged at dinner that night to answer the telephone. To my surprise I heard Valerie on the other end of the 'phone saying that she was at the Swiss/French border and that she realized that she had left her umbrella in the room she had occupied. She then asked if I really had meant a remark I had made that I often went to London and would be very pleased to see her there. Could I possibly look in the cupboard in her room to see if her umbrella was there, and if so, to eventually bring it to London and give it to her. Well, I am sure it was a put-up job!

I went to her room after dinner, found the umbrella, finished the holiday, went back to Eastbourne, and some time later when I was going to London to a meeting, I phoned her up and arranged to give her back her umbrella. On hearing that she lived opposite Kew Gardens, I think I am right in saying I arranged to take it to her home, and to meet her mother as well as returning the umbrella.

Later that year, Valerie suggested that I join her in another trip to St. Moritz where she had to visit various hotels in that area as it was her headquarters for the year. As I was then retired and free to do more or less as I wished, I gladly agreed to do this, and had a splendid fortnight being introduced to a lot of hoteliers and seeing another side of the skiing life as arranged through the Combined Services Winter Sports Association. After that our friendship continued, and she and her mother came to visit me in Eastbourne on more than one occasion, and I went up to town and stayed with them several times.

A friend of hers at the Combined Services Association was a Scot called Stuart Ferguson, who was director of a large pharmaceutical company in Scotland. He had taken up skiing late in life and became a first-class skier; we also met him at St. Moritz. It was suggested that he had a spare caravan on a site in the South of France, near St. Maxine, where he had a permanent double caravan for himself and his wife, and this spare one which he used to encourage his business staff to use as a holiday home. He invited us to take advantage of it, which we eventually did. This invitation was offered to us on more than one occasion and we had some marvellous holidays in the South of France.

We travelled by our own car, which was an Austin Maxi 1750, and we had a marvellous holiday in Macquis country about 15 kms North of St. Maxine. It required a planned visit to go down to the sea and bathe and we couldn't just have a bathe when we felt like it as if you lived on the sea front. I had bought the Maxi car second-hand through Caffyns of Eastbourne because it is the only car made where the backs of the front seat go absolutely flat on the rear seat and you can make space for two tall people to get into sleeping bags and stretch out full-length. Our luggage was in the boot in a separate compartment and so there was no interference. In that way we used to dispense with the need to use hotels and we had a meal whenever we felt like it.

The usual programme was to set off from Eastbourne to Newhaven in the early morning, to catch the first boat to Dieppe, and then travel by the side roads through the countryside and villages, and eventually getting down to the south coast of France. We never used any motorways and we just ambled along as we felt like it, picnicking when we felt the need, buying provisions as required, and about tea-time scouting around for a place to park the car comfortably and safely in the night hours. The location had to be level and preferably facing the east and the rising sun, but which also invisible from any road or farmyard. This we managed very successfully for many years. We had our main meal in the evening, choosing a hotel and the menu we liked best, and afterwards returning in our car to our selected spot. I must say we never had any trouble with any visitors, apart from a sheep or two, and we felt very secure. Breakfast consisted of a simple meal of Kelloggs cornflakes, with a pot of tea or coffee, which we made on our own portable stove, and we washed in our own basin with water from a big jerry-can which could be heated up quite easily. We were really quite self-contained.

In the caravan which was a big one on wheels, although static, we had everything fitted up, with a water supply and a toilet, with main drainage, as well as mains electricity, and this was very comfortable, and we looked after ourselves and did our own cooking unless we felt the need to go out for a change. Our host and hostess, Stuart and his wife Sybil, were our close neighbours but out of sight, and we never infringed upon each other unless by invitation. This happened frequently, and often we went out to dine together, or even entertained each other in one's own little area. Certainly sitting in the summer outside the caravan on a little patio, unseen by anybody else, and watching the sun setting, was absolutely marvelous.

There came a time when I tried to persuade Valerie to give up her splendid job as secretary to the Combined Services Winter Sports Association and marry me, and when she had thought it out well and truly, she decided that she would. After the marriage, which was on August 22, 1975, we went down to the South of France many more times.

All this time, Valerie and her mother used to come to Eastbourne fairly often and I took advantage of staying with them the odd night in London, especially when I had a meeting to go to, and I got to know her mother very well, as a charming lady, aged I think about 84 when I first knew her, but she walked me off my feet in Richmond Park even then. On one of these visits I was taken into Kew Gardens, which in those days you could enter for the princely sum of one whole penny, and it was nice to go in there after tea when most of the visitors had left for their own homes, and it was quiet and charming. I was introduced to Kew Gardens in a different way to what I had known before, but what interested me most was that while they could point out to me the famous tulip tree, both of them were rather ignorant about the names of other even relatively simple trees, like a plane tree, and of course this was due to the fact that they lived in a flat and had no garden. Although they liked looking at trees and shrubs, they were not particularly interested in their names.

We made many visits to the Gardens and to Richmond Park but I kept mum about the fact that when I had lived in the Willesden area, not only had the family paid regular visits to Kew Gardens by travelling down the North London railway line from Brondsbury Park to Kew Gardens, but in my school days we had always had our Officers Training Corps field days in Richmond Park, and so I really knew both of these places reasonably well, although I had not visited them for many years once I left London for Eastbourne. However, one day it came out that while they thought they had been introducing me to something quite new, I really was not playing very fair by pretending not to know anything about it all, and I got a good wigging for leading them up the garden path!

Touching the question of marriage, it meant that Valerie would not be able to carry on as Secretary to the Combined Services Winter Sports Association,

Presentation of plaque by Mayor, Councillor Leslie Mason, in recognition of Tom's work and his 50 years' service to the local Eastbourne community.

(l to r) Valerie, Lady mayoress, Tom, Mayor Leslie Mason, Sandra, Councillor Maurice Skilton, and Anthea at the Mayor's Reception.

The Order of St.John Investiture

10th September 1987

although we did consider that she might be able to do this from Eastbourne, and even have a special caravan in the garden as an office. But she decided, rightly I think, that being a housewife and secretary would not work, and so she had to resign. This was unfortunate for the Combined Services because her senior staff consisted of a very able and not-so-young woman who did all the costing, with a much younger and marriageable woman who could do the office work, but really had not any idea how to arrange contracts with the Swiss and to see to the overseas side. Of course the Services Association was run by the Admirals, Generals and Air Marshals and in rotation they elected one of them as chairman, but they themselves left all the work to the secretariat, and at this stage nobody gave any thought to how this Association was to be continued, and of course the next thing that happened quite obviously was that Valerie's No. 1 became engaged, was married soon afterwards and gave up the job, and there was nobody left who had any idea how to run the show. So it collapsed, which was a great pity.

At that stage it was taken over by the Royal Navy Ski and Winter Sports Association and all the records and things were handed over to them. They ran it as best they could, but that organization too decided to fold up and eventually the Combined Services Winter Sports Association came to a final stop.

From then on we went skiing, mostly at Flims, every

year until I began to get trouble in my left hip, and I think this was due to being knocked down the previous year high up the mountain by a gang of men on a huge toboggan who knocked me for six. After a few days I had the most marvellous bruising all down my left side from tummy to ankle, and I have got a coloured photograph of this somewhere for the record. I think this was the start of the trouble in the hip and eventually I had to give up skiing, but I did ski into my 80th year, going up the whole course to the top of the glacier and down again, and that was my final ski. Although I decided to go once more, the hip got so painful that I had to have something done and cancelled that trip. Instead, I had a hip replacement.

It so happened that at home Valerie fell down our front stairs and got a typical skiing ankle fracture, called a Potts fracture, and although she tried to ski again once after this mended, she couldn't get enough movement in the ankle and she too had to give it up. So that was the end of our skiing careers, which had been really quite marvellous.

In addition to going abroad, as a final word on skiing, whenever there was any snow in Eastbourne, which wasn't very often, we used to get our skis out, practice round the tennis court, and then get into the car and go to the top of Beachy Head and endeavour to ski home. It depended on the amount of snow how much pleasure you got out of it. Then later in the day we got the second car out and brought the first car home. This occurred three or four times before we had to give up skiing and was really quite a bit of fun.

One other point of interest is that since the Second War, twice in separate years we have had sufficient snow to make the Eastbourne roads impassable and all traffic brought to a standstill including the railways, and on these two occasions, I got my skis out and skied to and from St. Mary's Hospital over the golf course of the Royal Eastbourne Golf Club, and another trip down to the sea front and to the Esperance Nursing Home. That was the only means of getting there. I didn't see anybody else skiing; nobody took any notice and I might never have done it, but it was quite an experience. I think that is all I can remember about my skiing days, and I hope it gives you some idea of what a wonderful time I had.

Gladys Rolliston

As I have reported earlier on, I was billeted with a family called Rolliston at Hellingly Hospital in 1939 before going to the war, and I have also mentioned how kind they were in befriending the family who had to be evacuated to Harpenden as Eastbourne was a dangerous area for invasion.

Mrs. Rolliston, known as Gladys, and to us all afterwards as Auntie Gladys because the children called her that, continued the friendship after the war, and it has lasted until almost the present time. It wasn't long after we got back from the war that Mr. Rolliston retired from his post as secretary to the Hellingly Hospital, and he and his family moved to a new house in Upper Kings Drive, Eastbourne, which was splendid for us because it was only about three miles away. There they settled in with their son and daughter, Dave and Hazel. However it wasn't very long afterwards that Rollie, as he was always known, suddenly died while making a speech at some conference, and soon after that Gladys moved again to a bungalow in Polegate which the family found for her, because by that time both Dave and Hazel had been married, and they were living away from home. This bungalow was a very nice one on a new estate in Polegate, and this was only five miles away from us. The friendship continued, and she was a frequent and regular visitor to both houses in Eastbourne, and after Olive died, she took pity on me and used to come in at least once a week and do some cooking and cleaning up, and very often spent a night in Sandra's old room, especially in the winter. I used to fetch her and take her home the next day. This state of affairs went on until I eventually met and married Valerie, and while Gladys continued to come for a time, she herself got more elderly and she realized I think that I had a very good wife, and coming in to the do the cooking wasn't necessary any longer.

However, I used to keep in touch and go and see her regularly, but there came a time when, being well over 90, she began to lose her memory, because up to that date, she had been walking down to Polegate village itself to get her paper and groceries every day. When her memory started to go fairly suddenly and quickly, her son and daughter decided she could no longer look after herself and she was taken to a very nice care home in Gorringe Road, Eastbourne. And there, too, we visited her regularly until she died peacefully, aged 98.

90th Birthday – 28th November 1994

Some time ago my wife Valerie and I discussed the question of doing something special for this 90th birthday, but it seemed quite obvious that it was impossible to organize a party by ourselves because we are both involved in so many activities in the town and elsewhere that the party could not be kept to a reasonable number without offending somebody by not inviting them. Also Valerie, who has attacks of what is known as ME, can never be certain that she would be fit enough to act as hostess on any particular occasion, and so that was another reason for deciding against giving a party in Eastbourne to all our friends and acquaintances.

So we got in touch with the family and they agreed that the best thing to do was to have a party in Suffolk, where Anthea lives at Little Wenham, and this is an area and a place where other members of the immediate family can easily collect for a short time, apart from my son, Crichton, who lives and works in Montreal, Canada. So Anthea agreed to hold this gathering in November on the 26th, and it is hoped that all members of the family, including Crichton and his wife Christa from Montreal, and my brother Joe and his wife Mary from West Sussex, will be able to be present.

In the meanwhile, I have had some surprises. On 4th October at Ascot House, Eastbourne, we held a little party for the Ascot House tennis players which was not only to celebrate the end of the season, but also to welcome Kitty on her 85th birthday. This little party was held in the lounge and in due course, after a very pleasant tea party which was organized by Eric and Everal Grey and my wife, Valerie, Eric brought in a specially made cake, with candles alight, for Kitty, who blew out the candles and cut the cake.

To my surprise, when the toasts and the odd remarks had been made, Everal appeared from behind the screen with another cake with nine lighted candles on for me, to give me a small party for my birthday to come. In addition to the cake, they all gave me small presents, such as a spectacle case, a bar of Galaxy chocolate, and a new rain gauge to replace the broken one in the garden. This was all a terrific surprise, and I must say, very pleasant.

On 22nd October 1994, we were visited by Valerie's god-daughter, Vicky Parsons, and her husband,

Gerard, and two sons, Jonathan and Matthew, who had just returned from their work in Stuttgart, Germany, and had taken up residence again in Stony Stratford. They were having a long weekend in a caravan holiday park close to St Leonards-on-Sea, and were spending the best part of the day with us. To my surprise they suddenly produced some presents in the shape of the most marvellous plant in a pot, a lovely carnelian which would have pink flowers fairly soon by the look of it. I was also presented with a small Thomas-the-Tank engine from the two boys.

On the evening of 19th November 1994, we had our fourth Annual Dinner/Dance of the Eastbourne Branch of the Royal Army Medical Corps Association, which was held at the Glastonbury Hotel, Eastbourne. When the meal was over, the loyal toast was drunk, and other toasts were proposed by the Mayor and replied to by Major Hackett, followed by a toast to guests by the Honorary Secretary, Ron Collins, and replied to by The President of the Eastbourne Combined Ex-Services Association, Commodore J Derek Patterson, CBE, RD, RNR. Instead of going down to the ballroom for our dancing, proceedings were held up first by Capt Archer of the 217 General Hospital Territorial Army at Brighton, who made a short speech and presented me with a soft parcel with a few kind words to the effect that it was from the Brighton Company for my birthday present. I was encouraged to open it, which Valerie did for me, and there was a lovely blue coloured polo-necked sweater with a splendid logo on it with the remarks 'from the Brighton Company'. Then, secondly, Dr Kenneth Vickery stood up, and gave a long eulogy about my life with special reference to my service in the Territorial Army starting in the 1920's. Then, thirdly, Major Jimmy Howe, MBE, who had been a prisoner of war with me at Stalag 8B, Lamsdorf, Silesia, and who afterwards went up the ranks to finish up as Senior Band Master to the Guards Brigade, also gave a short talk about what it had been like in prison life, and how he had met me there, and how we had continued our friendship since. He said he was representing the Eastbourne Branch of the Dunkirk Veterans Association - of which he was the President. He then presented me with a beautiful illuminated shield carved in wood with the Dunkirk Veterans logo.

Having thanked these present-givers, I was told to sit down again and Ron Collins, our RAMC Branch Secretary, came behind me and said further kind words about our relationship, the formation of the local Branch of the RAMC Association, and how he was detailed to present me with a lovely silver salver from all the members of the Branch, and it had the following words engraved on its circular surface:

Presented to T. Henry Wilson OBE, O.St.J., TD, FRCS.
In warm affection by members of the Eastbourne Branch of
RAMC Association on the occasion of his 90th birthday 28th
November 1994

He then proceeded to tell the company that in his capacity as a master stonemason he had carved out a relief of my head and neck, side-view, on a marvellous piece of Welsh slate, and this had been encased in a lovely wooden frame which was put together by another friend of mine, Arthur Whatley, who lives in the Eastbourne Memorial Houses.

As you can imagine I was quite overcome by all these lovely gifts and was finally allowed to say a few words of thanks, after which we all proceeded to the ballroom, but a considerable amount of the dancing time had been taken up by this unexpected and very welcome end to the dinner.

Finally, before we left the room, a member of the hotel management staff came round with a specially made and enormous cake with suitable wording on the top -Happy Birthday - and nine lighted candles which of course I had to blow out in one big blow. So at last they were able to go and dance.

Further 90th. Birthday Celebrations

Now this story is the real story surrounding my 90th birthday. We were a big family party at my daughter Anthea's farmhouse at Little Wenham, near Ipswich in Suffolk.

We had decided to save our energy and go there by taxi and our driver was a well-known friend of ours,

Mr. Aspland. We set off from Ascot House about 9.30am on 24th November 1994, a Thursday. The weather was dull, windy but dry, and the drive was uneventful, but after we had gone through the Dartford tunnel, we stopped in the Thurrock Service area to have some light refreshments, and in fact we had a very nice mushroom cream soup. We then drove on to Great Dunmow and beyond that to another smaller village called Great Easton to call upon friends of mine, a Dr and Mrs Ian Graham who used to practise in Tiverton, Devon. Unfortunately he had a terrible stroke a few years ago and both he and his wife, Freda, had to live in a nursing home, and they elected on this one called The Moat House in Great Easton because it was near their daughter and other relatives. Unfortunately it so happened that Ian Graham had died a few days before our visit so we were only able to see Freda who looked better than I had seen her for many years, but was still an invalid confined to her chair or bed.

After that we continued on our way and finally reached Little Wenham and my daughter's house at 1.45pm where we were greeted with great enthusiasm, and all our luggage was taken to an upstairs bedroom.

At this stage there was only Anthea and her husband Giles, and Valerie and me in the house, apart from the dogs and cats. After tea and later supper, we all retired for the night.

On Friday 25th November, after breakfast, we set off to the East Anglian Agricultural showground near Ipswich to visit a craft fair, where we not only had a nice lunch, but the girls bought many articles. At teatime we were taken by Anthea down to see Debs and Georgina and Henry while Richard came in later, and we all had tea and watched the children making Christmas cards and playing with their jigsaw puzzles.

At this time my son Crichton and his wife, Christa, arrived from Montreal to join in the celebrations. They had actually arrived the day before by air but spent the previous night and most of the day visiting Cambridge where Crichton had been at Clare College. Also, during the evening, Anthea's two daughters, Jacqueline and Susannah, arrived to join the gathering, and some presents were opened.

Saturday 26th November was a quiet morning but after breakfast Sandra and husband Peter with the two boys, Mark and Neil, arrived in their caravan, after which we had a splendid sit down lunch in the dining room. I was careful not to eat too much as I knew we were having a party in the evening. At about 6 o'clock my brother Joe and his wife Mary, who live at West Chiltington, in West Sussex, arrived from the Posthouse Hotel where they were staying the night, and shortly before seven o'clock we all got into various cars and were driven to the market town of Hadleigh where we entered one of the old-fashioned houses in the main road which is called 'The Odds and Ends'. As you entered the hall of this old house, you turned right into a main room where there were several tables covered with cloths ready for a meal but no cutlery. This room led into the original kitchen with its old-fashioned coal stove. In these two rooms we gathered round talking and having our pre-meal drinks. By this time, Petrina and her husband Stephen also arrived to join the party, and everyone was present.

When the meal was ready we were all taken back to the hall and into the big room on the other side of the font door in the hall where tables were laid, six seats at each table, two tables lengthwise side by side, and the so-called top table at right angles to them both. We were given our seats and told to sit down and I, as the birthday boy, was seated in the middle of the top table facing everybody else. You will be able to see from the numerous photographs that were taken who was sitting at which table.

We had a marvellous meal of three courses, all delightfully what I would term 'home-cooked', but it was really a delicious meal, and it was accompanied by a wine of your choice. After the main course, all the ladies were asked to move around and take another place, so as to have someone else in the family to talk to. This was a very good arrangement. There was a menu of the sweet course only, which everybody signed for me to keep as a souvenir. When the meal was finally over and we had finished our coffee, Crichton got up (he was sitting in the far left-hand corner of the room) and made a splendid speech, I suppose you might call it, but in a very pleasant vein, talking about myself and the birthday party, and everybody present. He then produced a blue-carded file which had been cut in the shape of an oval on the front cover, behind which was fixed a picture of myself taken some years ago in the mess at Mytchett, Aldershot, in the Royal Army Medical Corps. Inside this file there was a beautifully printed four-page, foolscap-size paper on which had been printed an ode to me which he had written himself. This was really a very clever poem which covers my life from birth to the present day and includes all the main points in my life. At the end of this recitation, he came across and handed the file to me. At this stage he proposed a toast to me, and good health for the future.

I then rose myself and thanked him for this clever little speech and thanked everybody for coming to the party, mentioning that there were only two people missing from the party who had been at my 80th birthday and these two people were my brother William Hubert, and his wife Margaret, the reason being that he, poor chap, was not well. I then made a toast to all the family.

At this point my daughter Anthea got up and produced a big-looking book which she presented to me, and on the front page was written my name and *THIS IS YOUR LIFE*, in a similar way to that you can see on this programme on BBC 1 television.

On opening the pages, there are a series of photographs going right back to my early days and right up to date, but it is interesting to me that there are no pictures of my Army life, nor of my skiing holidays. But otherwise it is a marvellous collection covering the main points of my life.

I gather it was very difficult to collect a lot of these pictures because during the summer when all this was being worked on, I had decided to be a bit on the bad health side, and when I recovered enough to get out of bed, I spent most of the very hot summer keeping cool in the garden on the nice chaise-longue in the shadow of the bushes, and of course while I was home all the time, it was difficult to get telephone conversations and anything else going because I was always about. I generally had my portable telephone with me in case I had to answer it, so that, as well as the painting of the pictures which you will hear about also, it must have been quite a problem.

At this point, Crichton got up again and leaning behind into the corner of the room, he produced a big parcel, about 3 ft by 2 ft, beautifully done up in wrapping paper which must have been bought in Canada as it had the fleur-de-lys in gold on a blue background which is the insignia for the Province of

Valerie and Tom and the painting of Ascot House.

Tom and Crichton after Tom received his Ode.

Tom with his children *(l to r)* Sandra, Crichton and Anthea.

Quebec in Canada. He made a few remarks about the parcel and then came across, and was joined by Anthea to whom he gave the parcel. She, as No 1 in the family, gave it to me personally. I then had the pleasure of undoing the wrapping, and lo and behold, the inside consisted of a beautiful picture frame about the size I have already mentioned and in the frame was a delightful water colour painting of Ascot House as seen from the lower lawn. He then produced a second, similar, parcel and came and gave it to me himself, as No 2 in the family, and when I opened this, it was a similar matching frame with another water colour painting centered round our greenhouse or what is more commonly known as the conservatory. And finally, he produced a third and similar parcel, which he handed to Sandra, No 3 in the family, who presented it to me and on opening it, there was a third and matching frame with a water colour of the entrance gate to our little plot of ground. It was explained to me that these had been done by Crichton's friend, Andrew John Price, who runs Penn's Art shop in Eastbourne. These were all delightful and I particularly like his style of painting. The three of them made a marvellous present from the three branches of the family.

I think that at this stage we all started to do the rounds and talk to each other and eventually we moved back into the ante-room where we had first gathered. At this point I must mention that all the rooms were delightfully furnished and the walls particularly good with their pictures and curtains, and the walls themselves were to me a beautiful shade of what I would call orange. As there was a most marvellous video taken of this event, those who were lucky enough to see it were able to realize what a pleasant background to the whole evening there was.

On looking at the notes made by Valerie, it appears that we did not have coffee in the main dining room, but it was served so that we could help ourselves in the ante-room to which we had returned. In this room on one of the tables was suddenly produced a lovely birthday cake made by Debs in the shape of a tennis court, with a green top surface and a net and the markings, and a little cat specially made by Georgina. There were candles on the cake and of course I had to blow them out. After which photographs were taken and the cake was cut, and we all had some, and a lovely cake it was. Of course it wasn't a currant cake or a fruit cake because they all know that I don't like that sort of cake, so to me it was wonderful that it was plain Madeira inside.

During the course of the dinner and in the ante-room afterwards where the speeches were made, a video was taken on Anthea's camcorder, I think mostly done by Richard himself. Those of you who were lucky enough to be able to see this recording would be amazed what a marvellous picture he has made and how true are the colours and the features of everyone concerned. And so to Anthea and Richard I owe special thanks for making this birthday party a memorable event and a record for the family in the future.

We were all then driven back to our respective homes and eventually went to bed, after a marvellous day. The next morning, Sunday 27th November, we were up at a reasonable hour ready to welcome Joe and Mary who came in for coffee and a chat before driving back to West Chiltington. Not everyone was present because Anthea and most of the young folk had gone off early to Newmarket to another Craft Fair which I was told was bigger and better than the one we saw in Ipswich.

For lunch we were driven by Anthea to the Miles' domain of Petrina and Stephen and the three children, Rachel, Emily and Philip, where we had a great tea party round a big table, and were joined by Stephen's father and stepmother. After this we went back to Wenham for a light supper.

It was now Monday 28th November 1994 and this is my actual birthday date. After a leisurely start to the day, the girls and Crichton went shopping in a nearby village, and on their return, we all set off to lunch at a delightful old pub called 'The Beagle' in the village of Sproughton, where we had a super pub lunch.

Later in the day Crichton and Christa left to stay with

his friend, Brian Meaby, just south of London, and Debs and her family came to tea at Wenham. After a quiet early evening and a nice meal arranged by Anthea, we put on the video of the Royal Army Medical party we had earlier in the month in Eastbourne so that the family could see it.

On Tuesday 29th November we were collected by our driver and set off at 10 o'clock exactly to drive home, stopping at Shenfield to visit Valerie's god-daughter, Diane, and one of her two children, the other being at school and the husband at work. We should have seen them all on our way to Wenham the previous week but as the children had colds, and as we weren't very keen to catch them, we decided to postpone the visit until this day, but course missed seeing the whole family. Also there was Diane's mother, who is Valerie's schoolfriend Rosemary, who lives in Newcastle-upon-Tyne. So we were lucky to see her as well. After a lunch with them, we set off again and got back to Ascot House in Eastbourne at 3.45 pm. This was a memorable family reunion and we are hoping to repeat this in ten years' time when some of the youngsters will be old enough to join in, but it might be wise to think about one in five years' time!

But of course the whole festival, if you can call it that, hadn't ended here, because on the 30th November, Crichton and Christa re-joined us at Ascot House and stayed until the following Sunday morning, when they had to set off to Heathrow airport for Crichton's return to work at Montreal, and Christa to take another flight to Germany to spend a week with her family.

During these few days they popped in and out, visiting lots of their friends both in Eastbourne and further afield and we finished up with a splendid dinner party at the Lansdowne Hotel, just the four of us, on the Saturday night. There are many photographs which I have collected together in a separate album to match up with all the other records.

You might think that that would be the end of the birthday celebrations, but on Tuesday 6th December, at the monthly meeting of the Eastbourne branch of the Dunkirk Veterans' Association, I was asked to attend especially as the President, Jimmy Howe, wished to show to everybody the illuminated shield which he had previously presented to me at the Annual Dinner of the Royal Army Medical Corps Association.

And yet again, on 13th December, Valerie and I were invited to a little coffee morning party given by the Pidgeon family, Doreen, Cohn and son Mark. When we arrived at their house, we found the ground floor filled with people I knew well, mostly from the National Health Service Retirement Fellowship of which I was Chairman for five years, which post I had relinquished the previous Christmas, while still remaining a member. A little presentation was made to me and again a beautiful cake was produced with umpteen candles which I had to blow out. Pictures were taken and a few kind remarks were made.

During 1994, before my birthday, my wife Valerie had more or less completed arrangements for us to have a cruise on a ship starting from Bergen in Norway and going up the west coast to the Arctic Circle, but owing to my indisposition, this had had to be postponed, and we hope to be able to do this in 1995. This is not an ordinary cruise but we go on one of the working boats which set off each day from Bergen calling at all the villages and towns on the way up to the North Cape and back again to Bergen. We have decided on a particular vessel, the MS Vesteralen, which leaves Bergen on the 9th June 1995 on a scheme which on their brochure is described as Hurtigruten.

It is important to realize that this trip is a gift from Valerie to us both to celebrate my 90th birthday. What a gift, and I am so looking forward to doing this with Valerie.

Editor's Note:

They did make the trip a year later, and Tom thoroughly enjoyed it. Tom died March 26, 1999, of sound mind, and having played tennis up to his 93rd year.

The Editor would like to thank *The Times* and *The Daily Telegraph* for permission to reproduce the following obituaries from their papers.

Colonel Henry Wilson

Army surgeon who operated on sick and wounded PoWs in squalid German prison camp conditions

Wilson: great improviser

The Daily Telegraph of Monday, June 21, 1999

COLONEL T. HENRY WILSON

Colonel T. Henry Wilson, OBE, TD, surgeon and wartime medical officer, died on March 26 aged 94. He was born on November 28, 1904.

CAPTURED by the Germans in May 1940 at Boulogne, where he had elected to remain in charge of a hospital tending battle casualties, Tom Wilson spent the next five years working as a surgeon in prisoner of war camps. Operating in often primitive conditions, creating artificial limbs for amputees out of whatever materials came to hand, he cared for thousands of sick and wounded men, first at holding camps in Northern France and later at PoW camps in Germany.

A surgeon at Eastbourne in the prewar years, Wilson came to the RAMC via the Territorial Army into which he was commissioned in 1930. In January 1940 he went to France with the British Expeditionary Force and at the time of the German breakthrough in May that year was in charge of the hospital at Boulogne, where casualties rapidly mounted.

As it became clear that defeat stared the Allies in the face, he sent as many of his patients back to Britain as he could on any boat that became available. In the meantime, as the enemy drew near and shells fell around, he and his staff continued operating in a hospital whose windows had been blown out and which had no electricity.

He might have expected to be evacuated himself in due course. But when asked if he would remain behind to care for the wounded he unhesitatingly agreed. His medical unit was still carrying out operations at Boulogne when it was overrun by German troops on May 24, 1940.

After several moves, often having to care for patients in improvised surroundings in schools and churches in Northern France, Wilson was put in charge of all the serious surgical cases and sent to Germany, to a PoW camp in an old mental hospital at Hildburghausen in Thuringia. There for the next three years he tended wounded soldiers in the most rudimentary conditions, using primitive anaesthetics such as chloroform for operations.

From there in 1943 he was moved to Oflag IXC at Spangenburg near Kassel, an officers' camp where he was not allowed to work. This irked him and he agitated to be allowed to return to caring for the sick and wounded. The German authorities eventually capitulated and he was sent to Stalag VIIIB at Lamsdorf in Silesia.

There he found himself in charge of 20,000 men, mainly sick or wounded. Over the next two years he became a legend to his patients for the marvels of surgery he conducted in appalling conditions.

With the approach of the Russians early in February 1945 the Germans abandoned Lamsdorf. Wilson remained behind as the only surgeon, tending his patients until he and they were forced out of the camp at gunpoint by the SS and herded into cattle trucks for the long haul southwestwards to Memmingen in Swabia.

There they found themselves amid a multitude of prisoners and displaced persons of all nationalities, living in total squalor. Wilson and the British contingent of soldiers took charge of the situation and restored order and basic hygiene. Finally, on April 24, 1945, the PoWs' ordeal was over when the camp was liberated by the tanks of General Patton's US 3rd Army.

Returning to Britain on VE Day, Wilson later went back to Eastbourne where he was consultant surgeon to the Eastbourne Group of Hospitals from 1948 to 1969. He also became honorary surgeon to the British Limbless ex-Servicemen's Association and was medical officer to the Chaseley Home for severely injured and paraplegic ex-servicemen.

His enthusiasm for the Territorial Army continued unabated. In 1946 he had reformed the TA in East-bourne and was appointed CO of the 4th (Eastern) Casualty Clearing Station RAMC.

Wilson was a keen sportsman until late in life. Although he suffered a compound fracture of the leg while skiing in the 1950s, he made a full recovery and continued to ski until he was 80. He was also playing tennis until a few years ago. He was appointed OBE at the end of the war for his services to PoWs and also held the Territorial Decoration.

Tom Wilson is survived by his wife Valerie and by the son and two daughters of a previous marriage.

The Times, May 10, 1999

Notes about the Editor

Crichton Wilson is the son of Tom Wilson, and was born and bred in Eastbourne.

After studying at Eastbourne College and Clare College, Cambridge, he worked as an Engineer in the aircraft industry in England, until being offered work in Montreal, Canada in 1966, where he has lived ever since. Tom visited Crichton in Montreal several times, and the two of them had the opportunity to become very close.

After Tom's death, Crichton decided to put his story into electronic form, and later to publish it, especially after realizing the affection and respect Tom had earned in his life, as brought home by the wide range of people who took themselves to the Memorial Service held for Tom.

Editor's note regarding back cover:

When my father was a medical student and getting into surgery, he deliberately started doing heraldic embroidery as an exercise to improve his stitching skills.
When he was a POW, he continued to do some of this, partly to occupy time, and he made for my mother a beautiful petit-point evening purse.
Another example was the tapestry of a scene from a window at the Hildburghausen PoW camp in Thuringia, as shown here on the back cover.

He was also adept at knitting, and made a lovely Fairisle jumper for my mother, as well as making turtleneck sweaters for himself, using unwound wool from the white operating room socks supplied by the Red Cross.
Later, my mother taught him by letter to crochet.
After the war, my parents took me to London to see an exhibition of arts and crafts made by POWs, and several items from my father were shown there.

Lightning Source UK Ltd.
Milton Keynes UK
UKOW031150230911